United States

Paper Money Errors

A Comprehensive Catalog & Price Guide

3rd Edition

Dr. Frederick J. Bart

©2008 Frederick J. Bart

Published by

krause publications

An Imprint of F+W Media, Inc.

700 East State Street • Iola, WI 54990-0001
715-445-2214 • 888-457-2873
www.krausebooks.com

Our toll-free number to place an order or obtain
a free catalog is (800) 258-0929.

Library of Congress Control Number: 2008929071
ISBN-13: 978-0-89689-714-4
ISBN-10: 0-89689-714-1

Designed by Marilyn McGrane
Edited by Randy Thern

Printed in the United States of America

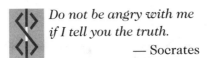

Do not be angry with me
if I tell you the truth.
— Socrates

Table of Contents

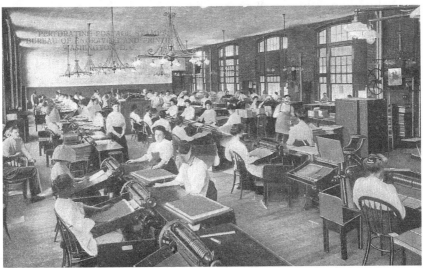

I had as many doubts as anyone else.
Standing on the starting line, we're all cowards.
— Alberto Salazar

PREFACE

Once considered an eccentricity, the subspecialty of United States paper money errors now stands rightfully alongside of other dominant market sectors. This field garners greater respect, stronger acceptance, and wider support than at any previous time. Such popularity has not escaped notice. Every generalized reference book on United States paper money now includes a chapter devoted to paper money mistakes.

Since the publication of the second edition, the largest collection of paper money errors ever formed crossed the auction block. The Taylor Family Collection was sold by Heritage-Currency Auctions of America in 2005. The catalogue provides an important resource. A smaller, but equally stellar collection—which had won the Peoples' Choice Award at the American Numismatic Association convention—was sold by Lyn Knight Currency Auctions.

The John Whitney Walter collection, sold in 2004, concentrated on breadth, rather than depth. The Taylor Family and John Whitney Walter auctions, along with other public sales, whet the insatiable appetite of the collecting community, which continues to devour the offerings and willingly pays higher prices.

The 3rd edition reflects ongoing research which began more than one-quarter century ago. This volume contains hundreds of new illustrations and data not previously available to enhance the knowledge base of collectors at all levels.

F.J.B.
Roseville, Michigan
April, 2008

*You're happiest when you're
making the greatest contribution.*
                    - Robert F. Kennedy

ACKNOWLEDGMENTS

A work of any magnitude requires the assistance of numerous persons to achieve fruition. The three editions of this book offer no exceptions.

Doris A. Bart made greater contributions to this edition than anyone else.

Aside from her unrelenting support, her technical prowess in generating scans, maintaining a library of images, and assisting with the layout enhanced the final product. Additionally, most of the illustrations of errors on the $2 denomination came from the reference collection of Doris A. Bart.

The nucleus of the illustrations in this volume is from the comprehensive collection owned by Gregg Anderson. Although there were numerous other sources of photographs, images from his collection appear in each chapter. Gregg Anderson is not only a contributor and a client, but a friend as well.

The author acknowledges the significant contributions by Harry E. Jones. He is truly the "Dean of Paper Money Errors." I am fortunate to be his student.

Countless numismatists made particular contributions to the first, second, and third editions of this book. Gratitude is extended to:

Michael J. Abramson
Rick Allard
Gregg Anderson
Rahal Arora
Billy Baeder
Willy Baeder
Aubrey Bebee
   (deceased)
Dave Berg
Stephen John Bierne
Joseph E. Boling
Carl Bombara

Q. David Bowers
Jason Bradford
Glen C. Burger
Ray Burns
Jennifer Cangeme
Gene Christian
Dennis Ciechna
Joel Cohen
Terry Coyle
A. P. Cyrgalis
Alex Delatola
John DeMaris

Thomas Denly
Michael Devlin
Dr. Gregory V. Dubay
Tom Durkin
   (deceased)
Keith Edison
Lawrence Falater
Lawrence C. Feuer
Don Fisher
Jim Fitzgerald
Kevin Foley
Dennis Forgue

Harry Forman
William Gibbs
Donald Gilletti
(deceased)
Len Glazer
Stephen Goldsmith
James Gunnis
(deceased)
Larry Hanks
Don Herrman
Gene Hessler
Donald Hitchcox
(deceased)
Lowell C. Horwedel
Peter Huntoon
Terry Jinright
Dustin Johnston
Jeffrey S. Jones
Glen I. Jorde
A.M. "Art" Kagin
(deceased)
Dr. Donald Kagin
Dr. Don C. Kelly
Laura Kessler
Lyn F. Knight
David Koble
Robert Kolasa
Robert Kravitz
Ed Kuzmar
Tom Kyzivat

Christopher LaBarre
George LaBarre
J. L. Laws
A. C. "Art" Leister
Scott Lindquist
Jess Lipka
Dr. Daniel J. McCarthy
(deceased)
Charles McGinnis
Rocky Manning
John Markis
Vin Marotta
Richard Merlau
David Messner
Allen Mincho
Michael Moczalla
P. S. Mullen
Dr. Richard J. Noble
Chuck O'Donnell
(deceased)
Dean Oakes
Michele Orzano
V. H. "Ossie" Oswald,
Sr.
Thomas Panichella
Tom Parr
Michael Payton
Alex G. Perakis
Stephen Perakis
James Polis

Michael Polizzi
Lou Rasera
William Reulbach
(deceased)
Kent Robertson
Edward Rothberg
John N. Rowe, III
Fred Rubenstein
Jeff Rubenstein
Murray Rubin
Sergio Sanchez, Jr.
Joe Sande
George Schweighofer
Mickey Shipley
Hugh Shull
James Simek
Steven M. Sullivan
Michael Tauber
Graeme Ton, Jr.
Peter Treglia
Katy Thamerts
Allan Teal
Daniel Tsao
Dr. John Vender
Raymond Wasosky
Mark Weglarski
Fred Weinberg
Gary Whitelock
John Whitney
Robert Wood

Personnel from the Bureau of Engraving and Printing provided invaluable assistance. Cecelia Hartfield, curator of its historical research center, Antoinette Perry, and Herbert C. Wheelock, Jr. offered information, illustrations, and insight into the production of paper money.

The author acknowledges, with gratitude, the permission extended by the Coin and Currency Institute, Inc. to use the Friedberg numbering system. The abbreviation "Fr-" indicates Friedberg numbers from Paper Money of the United States.

We are, each of us, angels with only one wing, and we can only fly by embracing one another.
- Luciona de Crescenzo

DEDICATION

Angels make the sweetest music. Their melodies soothe, stimulate, and support me.

I've let lyrics reflect my love for them.

I dedicate this book to my angels:

my wife, **Doris Ann Bartolomei,**
"I tip my hat to the keeper of the stars
He sure knew what he was doin'
When he joined these two hearts…
I know I don't deserve a treasure like you
There really are no words
To show my gratitude." [1]

my children, **Bianca Blair Bartolomei,**
Frederick Peter Bartolomei, and
Candace Lynn Bartolomei,
"Let me tell you a secret, about a father's love
I said daddies don't just love their children every now and
    then
It's a love without end, amen." [2]

my parents, **Peter Bartolomei** and **Dr. Margaret Bartolomei,**
"Dear Mom and Dad
Whatta ya know we made our dreams come true
And there are fancy cars and diamond rings
But you know that they don't mean a thing
Well they all add up to nothing compared to you
I still love you more than anything in the world." [3]

my brother, **Edward John Bartolomei,**
"Got a brother who's got my back
Lord knows I'm a lucky man." [4]

my step-son, **Daniel Lee Smith,**
"You've got so much up ahead
You'll make new friends
These are nowhere near
The best years of your life." [5]

my grandparents, **Fred "Dodo"** and **Mary "Nina" Colombo,**
   and **Alphonsina "Nona" Bartolomei,**
"He said his greatest contribution
Is the ones you leave behind." [6]

my grandchildren, **Riley Garrett** and **Clayton Lewis,**
"You're gonna wish these days
Hadn't gone by so fast
These are some good times
So take a good look around; [7]

and

   The previous collectors and dealers of United States paper money errors, who possessed the foresight and consideration to preserve their specimens for our enjoyment.

(1). *"Keeper of the Stars,"* K. Staley, D. Mayo, D. Lee
(2). *"A Father's Love,"* G. Strait
(3). *"Baby Girl,"* J. Nettles, K. Bush, K. Hall
(4). *"Lucky Man,"* D. Turnball, D. Cory
(5). *"Letter to Me,"* B. Paisley
(6). *"Small Town Southern Man,"* A. Jackson
(7). *"You're Gonna Miss This,"* A. Gorley, L. MIller

You can only lead others where you yourself are prepared to go.
- Lachlan McLean

FOREWORD

As difficult as it seems to understand, when I started buying and selling errors there was only one book on the *entire* field of paper money. A book on error notes would have sold less than one hundred copies, most of them to the author's family. However, I always believed that because of the uniqueness of error notes, they deserved their own reference. Writing such a book was always on my "to do" list.

Fred and I first talked about a book on United States paper money errors in the early 1980s. He began a studious pursuit of the topic, one which he continues, and the first edition was printed in 1994. Since that time, there have been numerous changes and this current book reflects those.

Although I began with error notes many years before Fred did, he took a more scholarly approach. I was happy to provide the foundation for his education. Over the years, I've learned as much from his books as he ever learned from me.

This current edition contains enough information to educate any collector, whether they're experienced or new to the field.

HARRY E. JONES

PROLOGUE

I hope you never lose your sense of wonder
You get your fill to eat but always keep that hunger
May you never take one single breathe for granted
And God forbid love ever leave you empty handed
I hope you still feel small when you stand beside the ocean
Whenever one door closes I hope one more opens
Promise me that you'll give faith the fighting chance
And if you get the chance to sit it out or dance
I hope you dance,
I hope you never fear those mountains in the distance
And never settle for the path of least resistance
Living might mean taking chances but they're worth taking
Loving might be a mistake but it's worth making
Don't let some helping heart leave you bitter
When you come close to selling out reconsider
Give the heavens above more than just a passing glance
And when you get the choice to sit it out or dance
I hope you dance,
I hope you still feel small when you stand beside the ocean
Whenever one door closes I hope one more opens
Promise me that you'll give faith the fighting chance
And when you get the choice to sit it out or dance
Dance, I hope you dance

-"I Hope You Dance"
Tia Sillers and
Mark Sanders

MACERATOR, U.S. TREASURY, WASHINGTON, D.C.   9627

PART ONE

INTRODUCTION

MODERN PAPER MONEY PRODUCTION

CONDITION AND GRADING

VALUES

RELATIVE RARITY INDEX

RESOURCES AND REFERENCES

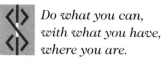

Do what you can,
with what you have,
where you are.
— Theodore Roosevelt

INTRODUCTION

Paper money began during the Yung Hui period of the T'ang Dynasty in China around 650-655. However, the first collectible note originated with the Ming Dynasty in 1368-1399. The Chinese issued the 100 cash denomination shortly after conquering the Mongols and forcing their retreat. The issue proved so excessive that most was recalled and destroyed. Available specimens surfaced between the boards in an attic over a generation ago.

Errors in printing probably predate the earliest known book, the Diamond Sutra, accomplished in China about 868. The Chinese and Japanese utilized carved wood blocks, to produce Buddhist charms, in the fifth century. In the 1100s, western Europeans initiated wood block printing to create playing cards and Christian illustrations. Leaflets and booklets printed from wood cuts contained predominantly pictures with limited words. These were painstakingly hand-copied.

The printing press evolved from the common wine press in the Rhine Valley region of Germany. Johannes Gutenberg, in 1440, introduced movable type which facilitated mass production. The original Gutenberg press contained hand-set characters, cut in relief, within a wooden frame. The surface of the characters received ink and the plate pressed against blank paper to impart an impression.

Printing technology evolved through the Renaissance era and Industrial Age, increasing the efficiency of mass production. *The Times*, a newspaper in London, England, initiated the use of a steam-powered press. Both the linotype and monotype machines, introduced in 1884 and 1897 respectively, facilitated type-setting. More recently, sophisticated soft-ware and advanced computers again revolutionized the speed and accuracy of mass production of the printed word and image.

The manufacture of United States paper money involves the application of an inked imaged onto currency stock. The paper undergoes multiple separate printing and cutting operations before release as individual notes. Since the introduction of non-metallic currency, collectors have

builtholdings for artistic, historic, sentimental, and investment purposes. Such collections exemplify the finest in workmanship. A parallel-and perhaps more eclectic-group of collectors has amassed examples of paper money exhibiting accidental mistakes. Such collections demonstrate the unusual and offer insight into the printing and production sequence.

Errors, misprints, oddities, freaks, or curiosities-regardless of the label-demonstrate a deviation from the intended finished product. Whether of human or mechanical causes, errors on paper money possess an appearance and appeal dissimilar to correctly printed notes. From the inconspicuous and insignificant to the monstrous and magnificent, paper money errors span a cosmic spectrum. Ink smears and double denominations anchor opposite poles in the range. This text illuminates each distinct type of error on United States paper money via information, illustrations, and offers "behind-the-scenes" insights and incidents.

*It is better to die on your feet
than to live on your knees.*
— Dolores Ibarruri

MODERN PAPER MONEY PRODUCTION

A true appreciation of United States paper money errors requires at least a cursory understanding of modern currency production. Paper money is prepared at the Bureau of Engraving and Printing (BEP) in Washington, D.C. and its satellite Western Currency Facility near Fort Worth, Texas which opened in 1991. A thumbnail examination of the sequence reveals that contemporary Federal Reserve notes (FRN) are printed via the dry intaglio method and completed on the currency overprinting and processing equipment (COPE or COPE-PAK).

The intaglio printing plates possess the skillfully engraved design incuse or etched below the surface of the steel plate. The intricate and masterful process deters counterfeiting because the procedure creates an embossed or raised impression which proves difficult to duplicate. Under terrific pressure, the sheet of currency stock is forced and squeezed into the recessed portions of the plate to capture the inked design. Prior to the development of modern inks and with less sophisticated equipment, the sheets were dampened prior to printing. The softened paper became more pliable and thereby maneuvered into the incuse regions with greater ease. Today, with the advent of improved ink and equipment capable of sustaining greater tons of pressure, the wetting has been eliminated. Sheets are dry when contacting the printing plate. The dry intaglio method reduces paper shrinkage and design distortion.

The BEP presently utilizes fully automatic, high-speed, sheet-fed currency presses that produce nearly 10,000 sheets per hour. Two presses operate in tandem. One press is responsible for generating back designs; the other simultaneously creates face printings. The Bureau blends dry colors, oils, and extenders in exact proportions to arrive at an ink which is virtually impossible to duplicate outside of government facilities. To minimize variation and ensure that all paper money matches in color and texture, each batch of ink undergoes extensive laboratory testing prior to use. Red and blue threads or fibers are embedded into the 75% cotton and 25% linen paper specially manufactured by Crane and Company of Dalton, Massachusetts. Under contract, the firm has supplied the Bureau with distinctive paper since 1879.

Since the series of 1990, a polymer security thread runs vertically within the substance of the currency stock. The thread is an integral part of the paper. Visible from both the front and back of the note, when held to a light source, the thread contains the denomination in numerical format alternating with the abbreviation USA. The polymer security thread feature appears on denominations between $5 and $100. Additional anti-counterfeiting measures, initiated with the series of 1990, include microprinting surrounding the portrait oval and magnetic ink in a checkerboard pattern across the face as part of the second print.

Effective with the redesigned Federal Reserve notes (FRN), which began with the series of 1996 $100 denomination-a watermark appears near the right end of the front. This feature appears on denominations between $5 and $100. The watermark reproduces the portrait image. The watermark appears invisible until the note is held to a light source. An additional anti-counterfeiting measure incorporates the use of color-shift ink in the lower right corner of the front. The ink rests atop an elevated, cross-hatched image of the numerals corresponding to the denomination. The ink appears to change color from black to green when the note rotates ninety degrees.

Effective with the series 2006 $5 denomination, the watermark was changed from that of the portrait to that of the denomination. Rather than seeing Abraham Lincoln when held to the light, a large numeral "5" appears. This eliminates the possibility of bleaching one design from a lower value and re-printing it with a higher denomination in an alteration outside the BEP.

The "Technicolor" series of notes began with the series 2004 $20. The multi-colored designs were then expanded to the series 2004-A $10, the $50 denomination, and the series 2006 $5. Eventually all denominations will include these anti-counterfeiting measures. It appears as though the use of color is only one aspect of many that the BEP anticipates incorporating to deter the distribution of bogus currency.

Contemporary United States paper money progresses through three distinctly different printing phases plus separate cutting operations.

Errors may arise at, or between, any point in the production. As currency designs continue to evolve and anti-counterfeiting measures continue to expand, there will likely be some variability to the basic stages outlined below.

First (back) printing: Each sheet of currency stock accepts an impression from a thirty-two subject printing plate bearing the back design. The plate contains thirty-two separate back designs, with each imparting the same back plate check number. The sheet passes between the engraved plate and an impression cylinder under tremendous pressure. The sheet remains untouched overnight, permitting the green ink to fully dry, prior to advancing to the second (face) printing.

Second (face) printing: This consists of the black portion of the face common to every FRN. These standard portions include the portrait, intricate outer border design of geometric patterns, series designation, and the engraved titles and signatures of the Treasurer of the United States and the Secretary of the Treasury. Effective with the redesigned paper money, a universal Federal Reserve seal is applied with the second printing. This generic seal appears on denominations from $5 through $100. The universa seal no longer cites the city and state of the issuing Federal Reserve bank.

As they leave the second printing press, sheets are sliced into sixteen subject half-sheets and are passed through two inspection stations. Prior to reaching the second station, mechanical arms flip over the sheets. Those passing inspection are trimmed to a standard size, piled into stacks of 10,000 half-sheets on pallets, and advanced to the COPE presses for the application of serial numbers and seal(s).

Third (over) printing: This final stage includes the non-intaglio printing on the front. This bi-color overprint imparts the green Treasury seal and the two sets of serial numbers. In some instances, the Treasury seal may be applied independently of the serial numbers. On the $1 and $2 denominations, the black portion consists of the Federal Reserve bank seal and corresponding district number. On the $5 through $50 denominations, an alpha-numeric combination-situated beneath the upper left serial number-indicates the issuing Federal Reserve bank. The currency overprinting and processing equipment contains built-in electronic and photoelectric sensors that interrupt the operation when it detects a mistake.

This automated stage eliminates the need for additional BEP personnel.

After completing the COPE process, the half-sheets are stacked into piles of one hundred consecutively numbered bills. Each stack of one hundred is banded into a "pack." Forty such packs are compressed, strapped together, and sealed into a "brick" within plastic shrink wrap. The bricks become packaged for shipment to and distribution from one of the twelve Federal Reserve bank or one of the twenty-four Federal Reserve bank branches.

Web notes: Although the sheet fed system again accounts for all paper money produced by the United States of America, in the recent past the BEP also utilized web fed presses. The Alexander Hamilton web fed system was purchased from the Stevens International, Inc. at a cost of $12.5 million. The system yielded over 17,000 sheets per hour, versus the 8,000 sheets effected by the traditional method. The web fed system drew a continuous roll of currency stock through a press that prints both the face and back of the note in a single pass. The printing plate was a chrome-plated copper cylinder with 96 intaglio images. Overprinting was accomplished on the standard COPE equipment. The web presses printed a distinct subset of $1 FRN for the series of 1988-A, 1993, and 1995.

Notes printed on the web fed press started in May, 1992 with the B-L block of the series of 1988-A. Delivery of the first web notes, to the Federal Reserve Bank of New York, occurred on June 15, 1992. Shortly thereafter, citizens began voicing complaints concerning the poorer quality products entering circulation. During a life span encompassing three series, host notes produced on web presses gave rise to twenty-two blocks including the series of 1988-A F-*. Although not intended to serve as star or replacement notes, 640,000 pieces were overprinted as such. Current estimates suggest that approximately 160,000 notes were released into circulation. The web fed press-criticized for inferior quality, crippled by mechanical problems, and fraught with an excessive spoilage rate (28% versus 6% on the sheet fed presses) was discontinued. In October, 1997 the BEP sold the press, after extracting the printing plates, for scrap metal value.

Minor variances differentiate web fed notes from those produced on sheet fed presses. The plate location check number was removed from the upper left of the front, as was the plate location check letter before the plate number at the lower right of the face. On the back, the check plate number was relocated from the lower right to alongside of the motto.

Future changes: As this book nears completion in 2008, several officials from the BEP confirm that designs on United States paper money will reflect a dynamic process. They indicate that additional design changes and anti-counterfeiting devices will continue, with major revisions likely in the foreseeable future. The recent past has seen the introduction of EURion constellations on the multicolored $10, $20, and $50 denominations. These represent patterns designed to "lock-up" photocopying machines and photo-editing software to thwart photographic reproduction as a means to duplicate and counterfeit currency.

Additional design changes could encompass as many as ten individual processes to further enhance the anti-counterfeiting features. Such measures might include the use of a hot stamp press to apply foil overlays, coating machinery to apply invisible ultraviolet ink, and a screen press to impart a raised design atop the surface of the currency stock.

Undoubtedly, numerous changes and refinements will occur prior to the forthcoming overhaul in designs. Concurrent with the changes will be the potential opportunity for heretofore unknown varieties of errors.

*Quality is like buying oats. If you want nice,
clean, fresh oats, you must pay a fair price.
However, if you can be satisfied with oats
that have already been through the horse...that comes a little cheaper.*

- unknown

CONDITION and GRADING

The state of preservation will, to a certain extent, affect the desirability and consequently the value an error note commands. Values of the more readily available mistakes remains strongly influenced by the note's condition or grade. A "common" error-if any error on United States paper money rightly can be referred to as common-such as a minor ink smear or single gutter fold carries minimal premium above face value in a circulated grade. On the other hand, a substantially rarer variety such as a multiple printing or major printed fold will retain much of it's premium even if the note is no longer new. A double denomination in any grade would be much more welcome in nearly every collection than a stack of crisp uncirculated notes with minor errors.

The grading of paper money is a subjective art, not an exact science. As such grading can evoke dispute and controversy but, seems important to some extent to all collectors. Although an exhaustive discussion of grading paper moneyss falls beyond

the scope of this book, a brief review of the criteria for the most popular grades appears appropriate and necessary. The descriptions here are adapted from The Comprehensive Catalog of U.S. Paper Money by Gene Hessler and used with permission of the author and BNR Press of Port Clinton, Ohio.

Special considerations apply to the evaluating and grading of error notes. In particular, folds, tears, and other mishaps which create the error must be ignored in assigning a grade.

Crisp Uncirculated (CU). Notes qualify for the CU designation only when they remain in the same condition as issued. The paper must be firm and crisp. Any indication of mishandling, counting marks, corner tip folds or corners no longer sharp and square must be mentioned in the description.

About Uncirculated (AU). Notes that appear to be in crisp uncirculated condition but, after close examination reveal minute signs of handling. These findings might include a center fold.

Extra Fine (EF). Notes in this condition will still be crisp. There will be evidence of handling, such as minor creases and folds. Corners begin to lose their squared edges. Traditionally, three folds defines this grade.

Very Fine (VF). Notes with moderate circulation that retain some crispness but, exhibit several folds and creases. Signs of handling should be anticipated. No tears on the edges are permitted. The corners begin to assume a rounded appearance.

Fine (F). Notes which begin to feel soft or limp typify the grade. The paper demonstrates countless folds, creases, smudges, minor edge tears, and colors that are starting to fade.

Very Good (VG). Notes which are heavily circulated often grade Very Good. These pieces may contain tears, thick or extensive smudges, faded colors, and heavy creases or folds. These creases or folds might cause a separation of the paper in the center of the note. Notwithstanding the folds, the note must be intact.

Good (G). Notes in this condition will exhibit blemishes as described for the condition of VG, only more severe. Corners of the note might be missing from wear.

Insights and Incidents. The proliferation of third-party grading companies has placed an unforeseen twist on the "importance" of condition. For nearly a century, collectors of paper money errors were satisfied with describing their note first as "Uncirculated" or "New" and later as "Crisp Uncirculated." The error was of primary importance, while the nuances of grading took a distant back seat. With the advent of independent grading services, there seems to be a suggestion of superiority when one example earns the grade of Gem Crisp Uncirculated MS-65 and another merits "only" Choice Crisp Uncirculated MS-64. Although this trend is likely to continue, it seems to undermine the fundamental reason why people collect paper money mistakes.

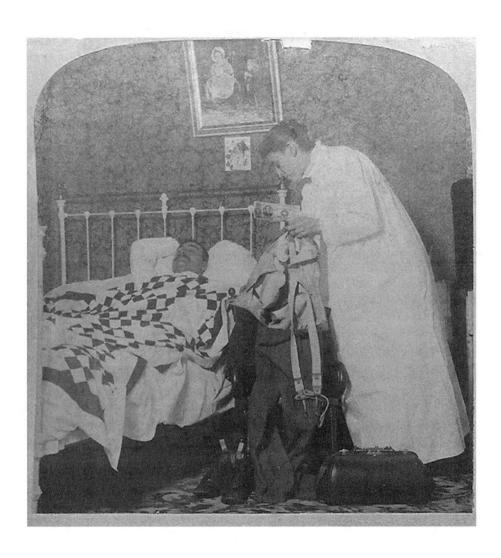

Try not to become a man of success,
but a man of value.

- Albert Einstein

VALUES

The value an error note commands reflects several factors: its condition, relative rarity, eye-appeal, popularity, denomination, and availability. Estimates are provided for the grades of fine, extra fine (EF), and crisp uncirculated (CU). It appears unnecessary to provide value guidelines for each level of CU. In those instances where a value is omitted, the error remains generally unknown in that particular state of preservation.

Where illustrated notes are unique or nearly so, such designators appear rather than hypothetical valuations. Such mistakes appear for sale so infrequently that on most occasions the previous sales record is shattered in response to an ever-increasing demand against a fixed supply within a dynamic market.

The value estimates throughout this book follow careful analysis of auction sale records, private transactions, dealers' advertisements and price lists, internet auction sales, consultation with prominent collectors and dealers, and the author's intimate involvement in the field of paper money errors for more than twenty-five years. The values—while not perfect—attempt to accurately reflect the current marketplace at the time of publication. Their accuracy will likely succumb to the passing of time.

Familiarity breeds contempt,
while rarity wins admiration.
- Apuleius

RELATIVE RARITY INDEX

The relative rarity index, developed by the author and initially presented in the first edition, places errors on small size Federal Reserve notes (FRN) and silver certificates (SC) into nine separate categories. An updated and refined index appears here.

The groups-each identified by a relative rarity [R] number-are arranged from R-1, the most common, through R-9, the extremely rare. Unlike most rarity rating systems which rank items according to the number of pieces hypothesized to be in existence, the following table provides a relative scaling of errors. The mistakes in a given rarity category are of similar scarcity. In this instance, errors are relatively rarer than those in the preceding (lower) R groups and relatively commoner than those in the succeeding (higher) R groups.

After examining literally thousands of major and minor mistakes on small size notes, during a twenty year timeframe, the author believes that errors appear with comparable frequency on FRN and SC. The relative rarity index was formulated with this consideration in mind. Errors on fractional currency, large size notes, and other classes of small size paper money (national currency, Federal Reserve bank notes, gold certificates, and United States notes) appear too sporadically to be meaningfully included in the guide. Similarly, the relative rarity index only reflects the status of regular issue notes. Star or replacement notes, because of their limited production, $2 FRN, and notes produced on the web press move into the next higher R group. Two dollar replacement notes move up two groups; likewise, one dollar web note stars. However, in no case may a rarity greater than R-9 be assigned.

R-1

- gutter or interior fold, single
- ink smear, small
- offset, partial
- overprint shift, minor
- partially turned or rolled digit

R-2

- face on back offset, complete
- faulty alignment, minor
- ink smear, moderate
- insufficient ink overprint, single digit
- overprint shift, moderate

R-3

- back on face offset, complete
- board break, small
- gutter or interior fold, large or multiple
- insufficient back ink
- obstructed print, small or moderate
- overprint shift, one color
- partially turned or rolled block letter
- solvent smear

R-4

- board break, large or multiple
- cutting error, minor
- engraving errors:
    - $1 1981-A back plate 129
    - $1 1985 back plate 129
    - $1 1995 micro 295 back plate
- faulty alignment, moderate
- ink smear, major
- insufficient face ink
- insufficient ink overprint, complete
- overprint shift, major
- mismatched serial numbers:
    - $1 1957 G 54xx/G 55xx
    - $1 1957-B U 37xx/U 47xx
    - $1 1969 F 68xx/F 67xx
    - $1 1981-A F99xx/F98xx
    - $2 1976 xx523 A/xx623 A
    - $5 1977-A L 44xx/L 45xx
- missing color shift ink
- missing district seal, series 1996 or later
- missing magnetic ink, partial
- missing overprint, one color
- printed fold, minor
- stuck digit

R-5

- cutting error, moderate
- inverted overprint, Type I
- inverted overprint, Type II
- mismatched serial numbers (other than those in R-4)
- missing magnetic ink, complete checkerboard pattern
- obstructed print, major or multiple
- overprint on back
- printed fold, moderate
- stuck block letter
- transposed currency stock

R-6

- cutting error, major
- double print, partial
- faulty alignment, major
- inverted "back," Type I
- mismatched block letters, including $2 1976 H-A/B-A
- missing first print (blank back)
- missing overprint

R-7

- double or multiple first print
- double or multiple second print
- inverted "back," Type II
- inverted block characters
- overprint offset on back
- printed fold, major

R-8

- double or multiple third print
- end of roll error
- engraving errors (other than those listed in R-4)
- missing second print
- overprint on back, inverted

R-9

- double denomination
- mixed denomination set
- obstructed print with retained fragment
- pre-printed stock
- printed scrap
- wrong stock error

*The few who do are the envy
of the many who only watch.*
- Jim Rohn

RESOURCES and REFERENCES

AUCTION HOUSES

The following firms frequently sell paper money errors via public auction:

Bowers and Merena, 18061 Fitch, Irvine, California, 92614

Early American History Auctions, P.O. Box 3341, La Jolla, California, 92038

Heritage-Currency Auctions of America, 3500 Maple Avenue, 17th Floor, Dallas, Texas, 75219

Lyn F. Knight, P.O. Box 7364, Overland Park, Kansas, 66207

R. M. Smythe, 26 Broadway, New York, New York, 10004

Spink America, 55 East 59th Street, New York, New York, 10022

Stack's, 123 West 57th Street, New York, New York, 10019

PERIODICALS

The following journals occasionally publish articles of interest to the collector of paper money errors:

Bank Note Reporter, Krause Publications, 700 East State Street, Iola, Wisconsin, 54990

Coin World, Amos Press, P.O. Box 150, Sidney, Ohio, 45365

Numismatic News, Krause Publications, 700 East State Street, Iola, Wisconsin, 54990

Paper Money, Society of Paper Money Collectors, P.O. Box 793941, Dallas, Texas, 75379

The Numismatist, American Numismatic Association, 818 North Cascade, Colorado Springs, Colorado, 80903

REFERENCES

Azpiazu, Robert, *The Collectors Guide to $1 FRN's Series 1963-2003A*.First City by PIP Printing, St. Augustine, Florida, 2005.

Bart, Dr. Frederick J., *United States Paper Money Errors,* 2nd Ed. Krause Publications, Iola, Wisconsin, 2003.

Bart, Dr. Frederick J., *Comprehensive Catalog of United States Paper Money Errors*. BNR Press, Port Clinton, Ohio, 1994.

DeLorey, Thomas and Reed, Fred, *Price Guide for the Collector of Modern United States Paper Money Errors*. Amos Press, Sidney, Ohio, 1977.

Donlon, William P., *United States Large Size Paper Money 1861 to 1923.* 6th Ed., Kagin's, Inc., Des Moines, Iowa, 1979.

Friedberg, Milton R., *The Encyclopedia of United States Fractional and Postal Currency*. NASCA, Long Island, New York, 1978.

Friedberg, Robert, *Paper Money of the United States*. 18th Ed., Coin and Currency Institute, Clifton, New Jersey, 2006.

Hessler, Gene, *The Comprehensive Catalog of U.S. Paper Money.* 5th Ed., BNR Press, Port Clinton, Ohio, 1993.

Huntoon, Peter and VanBelkum, Louis, *The National Bank Note Issues of 1929-1935*. Society of Paper Money Collectors, 1973.

Kelly, Don C., *National Bank Notes A Guide with Prices*. 5th Ed., Paper Money Institute, Inc., Oxford, Ohio, 2006.

Krause, Chester L. and Lemke, Robert F., *Standard Catalog of United States Paper Money*. 23rd Ed., Krause Publications, Iola, Wisconsin, 2004.

Kvederas, Bob Jr. and Kvederas, Bob Sr., *The Alexander Hamilton Web-Fed Press,* 2nd Ed. RAK Ink, Titusville, FL, 2004.

Murray, Douglas D., *Complete Catalog of United States Large Size Star Notes 1910-1929*, 3rd Ed. Coin and Currency Institute, Clifton, New Jersey, 2007.

O'Donnell, Chuck, *The Standard Handbook of Modern United States Paper Money*. 6th Ed., Harry J. Forman, Inc., Philadelphia, 1977.

O'Mara, Tom, *"Fractional Currency Inverts" in Paper Money*, Society of Paper Money Collectors, 208:99, 2000.

Schwartz, John and Lindquist, Scott, *Standard Guide to Small-Size U.S. Paper Money 1928 to Date*. 8th Ed., Krause Publications, Iola, Wisconsin, 2008.

Rothert, Matt, *A Guide Book of United States Fractional Currency*. Whitman Publishing Co., Racine, Wisconsin, 1963.

Shafer, Neil, *A Guide Book of Modern United States Currency*. 8th Ed., Whitman Publishing Co., Racine, Wisconsin, 1979.

Sullivan, Stephen M., *US Error Note Encyclopedia*. Capital Currency, Melbourne, Florida, 1997.

U. S. BUREAU OF ENGRAVING AND PRINTING.   Counting and Packing Currency for Shipment.

PART TWO

FIRST and SECOND PRINTING ERRORS

BOARD BREAKS

DOUBLE DENOMINATIONS

FAULTY ALIGNMENTS

INK SMEARS

INSUFFICIENT INKINGS

INVERTED BACKS

MISSING PRINTINGS

MULTIPLE ERRORS

OBSTRUCTED PRINTINGS

OFFSET PRINTINGS

Mistakes are the portals of discovery.
-James Joyce

BOARD BREAKS

The designation "board break" refers to the error resulting from a partially broken impression cylinder. An impression cylinder forces the unprinted currency paper into the intaglio recesses of the printing plate. The impression cylinder, or rigging, carries a wooden external wrapper; rigid enough to ideally sustain the workload yet pliable enough to squeeze the currency sheet into the plate.

The plate cylinder contains two or four thirty-two subject engraved printing plates. During the production of United States paper money, the currency sheet passes between the plate cylinder and the impression cylinder under 40 to 80 tons of pressure. Because the impression cylinder must endure such extreme pressure, areas occasionally become fatigued. The end result of such fatigue is failure as segments either compress into the cylinder or fall away. The disruption in the continuity of the impression cylinder yields an area incapable of pushing the currency paper into the incuse design on the plate cylinder. This produces a white unprinted area on the finished piece of paper money that correlates directly to the portion of the plate cylinder opposite the broken segment of the impression cylinder. Consequently, every note printed using the imperfect impression cylinder will exhibit the identical error-matching in size, shape, and

and location-unless the defect expands and/or until the rigging is replaced.

Typically, board breaks occur at a single location, are fairly small, and are discovered on numerous consecutive notes. However, regardless of the size or singularity of the error, the consistent characteristic is irregular, jagged margins surrounding the unprinted white void.

Fractional notes. At the dawn of the Civil War, the United States found itself in a precarious situation when fearful citizens began hoarding coinage because of the intrinsic metallic content. A shortage arose quickly and making change in commerce became extremely difficult. Although several temporary remedies arose (private scrips, tokens, checks, credit slips, and postage stamps), none proved satisfactory. The government introduced fractional currency to alleviate the shortage. The Treasury Department released 23 separate designs over five different issues. Although this class of paper money enjoys its share of errors, the board break is not among them.

Large size notes. Absolute proof that a board break actually exists on large size paper money remains absent. A couple of "curious freak" notes - as errors were formerly designated-described as being printed from broken plates appeared without photographs in auction sales catalogues in the first half of the 1900s. One piece was described as a series 1923 $1 silver certificate with the signatures of Speelman-White; the other, a series 1907 $5 United States note carried the same signature combination. The whereabouts of the particular notes remains unknown. Consequently, inspection is impossible. Alternatively, the authenticity of the items may since have been disproven or the etiology of the mistake ascribed to an alternate cause. No collector or dealer has reported the existence of a board break error on any large size note in recent times.

Small size notes. Federal Reserve notes (FRN), especially those after the 1963 series, hold most of the board break errors. Small runs of board breaks exist on virtually every series. The error appears on notes from every Federal Reserve district. The majority appear on the $1 denomination. Although, documented examples survive on every denomination of FRN through $100. Typically, board break errors affect a single location; nonetheless, a batch of $20 FRNs bearing at least three separate defects was reported by the author. A smattering of board breaks occurred on United States notes (most notably the $2 series 1953-B) and silver certificates. The lone example reported on a small size $5 National Currency represents an alteration; none are known on this class of paper money. The error remains unknown on gold certificates and Federal Reserve bank notes.

Insights and Incidents. The current focus in error collecting-which began in the mid-1990s-leans towards visually spectacular pieces. The hum-

ble board break, despite its relative scarcity, generates little excitement. Consequently, from a monetary perspective, board breaks appear to be among the most underpriced errors in the present marketplace.

An excellent group of multiple board breaks on series 1995 $2 FRNs from the Atlanta district surfaced in 1996. These offered collectors the premiere opportunity to acquire this error on a denomination infamous for a paucity of misprints. Initially, the pieces traded wholesale at forty dollars each; the immediate aftermarket witnessed retail sales around seventy-five dollars. However, after auction prices neared two hundred dollars, the price-not necessarily the value or scarcity-rose dramatically.

Surprisingly, another small batch of board breaks came to light on the two dollar denomination. Although discovered later, this group originated with the inaugural series of the bicentennial design. These series 1976 errors, from the Richmond district, exhibit cloud-like defects in the upper left region of the back design, printed with check plate number 1. When the author brought these to the market, savvy collectors purchased an example, the less experienced simply yawned at the chance.

A collector of even limited means can assemble a grouping of legitimately scarce error notes by concentrating on board breaks. Offerings remain few and far between. In fact, in assembling images for the 3rd edition of this book, locating examples of the board break error to illustrate proved more problematic than most every other category.

EXAMPLES OF THE ERROR

MINOR

MODERATE

MAJOR

$1   SC   1935-D   Board break; major   R-4
        Fine: $75   **EF: $150**   **CU: $250**

$1   FRN   1969   Board break; moderate   R-3
        Fine: $50   **EF: $75**   **CU: $150**

$1   FRN   1969-C   Board break; minor   R-3
        Fine: $25   **EF: $50**   **CU: $75**

$1	FRN	1969	Board break; moderate		R-3
	Fine: $50		EF: $100	CU: $150	

$1	FRN	1977-A	Board break; minor		R-3
	Fine: $25		EF: $50	CU: $75	

$1	FRN	1995	Board break; major		R-4
	Fine: $100		EF: $200	CU: $450	

$2	USN	1953-A	Board break; moderate	
	Fine: $150		**EF: $250**	**CU: $350**

$2	FRN	1976	Board break; multiple	R-5
	Fine: $100		**EF: $200**	**CU: $300**

$2	FRN	1995	Board break; multiple	R-5
	Fine: $100		**EF: $200**	**CU: $350**

$5	FRN	1988-A	Board break; multiple	R-4
	Fine: $75		EF: $150	CU: $250

$20	FRN	1977	Board break; moderate	R-3
	Fine: $50		EF: $100	CU: $150

$100	FRN	1990	Board break; moderate	R-3
	Fine: $150		EF: $200	CU: $250

Every great mistake has a halfway moment, a split second when it can be recalled and perhaps remedied.

- Pearl Buck

DOUBLE DENOMINATIONS

The double denomination reigns supreme among paper money errors. No other mistake conjures the romance, mystique, and fascination of the double denomination. In fact, across the entire spectrum of paper money collecting, very few notes can equal the allure of the two-value oddity. More publicity and lines of catalogue descriptions are showered upon the double denomination than any other misprint.

The double denomination note-with the face and back each representing a different value-happens in a rather simple manner. After a currency sheet receives the back printing of one denomination, the sheet enters the face and overprinting operations for another denomination. The confusion presumably arises during the transportation of the currency stock to the second printing stage, after a storage period subsequent to the first printing.

Depending upon the orientation of the note, the error is either blatantly obvious or totally obscure to the viewer. When both sides of the notes are visible, as in turning a page in a book, the disparity in denominations is readily apparent. However, when either side is viewed independently no error shows, as each side is perfect unto itself.

Fractional notes. Until the recent past, genuine double denomination errors on fractional currency remained unverified. Notes advertised or catalogued as double denomina-

tions were later proven to be skillfully adjoined fiber paper notes of different face and back values. However, a couple of fractional currency pieces have appeared at public auction bearing every conceivable characteristic of a genuine double denomination.

The notes, in crisp uncirculated condition, possess complete untrimmed margins and perfect alignment of the designs. The edges demonstrate no evidence of tampering. Additionally, the texture felt appropriate for the issue.

Large size notes. In sharp contrast to most errors, particularly the more profound mistakes, the double denomination exists in more varieties on large size paper money than on small size. National currency accounts for most of the double denominations. These represent all three charter periods. Notes from fourteen states and one territory were affected, providing unusual geographic diversity. A factor contributing to the large number of double denominations known on large size national currency is the sheet layout employed for some issues. In many cases, the uncut sheet contained two denominations. Examples are the $1-$1-$1-$2 format, the $10-$10-$10-$20 arrangement, and the $50-$100 set up. Therefore, if such a sheet was inverted for the face printing, the top and bottom notes became double denominations. Another contributing factor to the occurrence of double denominations on national currency is the large number of national banks (over 14,000 in total) mandating an astounding number of short printing runs at the Bureau of Engraving and Printing.

Large size paper money was printed in uncut sheets of four notes. Consequently, a double denomination error involving a single sheet produced a mere handful of notes. The only large size double denomination available with regular frequency is the $2 face/$1 back Federal Reserve bank note from the series of 1918. It occurred on at least three districts. Specimens of this two value misprint cover all states of preservation from the well-worn through crisp uncirculated.

Several examples of double denominations for the series 1914 FRN exist. These are known in two varieties: $20 / $10 and $5 / $10 from the Chicago district. Research by the author confirmed that all examples arose from $10 sheets printed by the same back plates, bearing check number 176.

Small size notes. The double denomination-aptly regarded as the "King of Errors"-remains the most pursued and coveted paper money mistake. Approximately 200 double denomination notes, representing four face/back combinations, are believed to exist. Of these, the $5 face/$10 back from the series of 1934-D Federal Reserve note from the Kansas City district provide the preponderance.

The first edition of this book observed "If additional double denominations do not develop, the upward spiral in value in response to an increasing demand for this spectacular oddity will almost surely continue." Prices have advanced by five- to ten-fold since those words were published in 1994!

Another speculation presented in the first edition, shortly after the polymer security thread became an integral part of counterfeit detection on United States paper money, "The potential for a new type of double denomination note now exists. Conceivably, a sheet of currency paper with security threads of one denomination could be printed by face and back plates of a different denomination, giving rise to a new hybrid." Presently a single documented example exists of series 1995 $1 FRNs from the Dallas district containing a partial embedded security thread from the ten dollar denomination. There are unconfirmed reports of two $1 series 1995 notes from Chicago bearing complete security threads from the ten dollar denomination.

A sub-type, the double denomination offset, has produced two confirmed examples. Each is a series 2003 $10 carrying an offset of the gold color-shift ink showing the denomination indicator "20" and the shield from a series 2004 $20. Bureau of Engraving and Printing (BEP) records indicate that each was produced during the same month.

Whether the BEP will accommodate the enormous demand for double denomination errors by accidentally producing more in the future remains open to conjecture.

Insights and Incidents. Perhaps the greatest discovery in the entire field of United States paper money errors, since the publication of the 2nd edition, is the identification and authentication of the very first double denomination printed by this country. Issued by the Second National Bank of Springfield, (MA), the $10 face / $20 back originates from the Original (1865) series of national banknotes.

Despite its low grade, the historical significance is not lost.

At the time of publication of the first edition, the probability of any United States paper money error garnering in excess of fifty thousand dollars, within five years, seemed improbable. However, if forced to speculate on which variety might first reach such a lofty level my initial guess would be an extremely rare $100 face/$50 back or $50 face/$100 back large size national currency double denomination. My intuition was partially correct: honors for the first paper money error to surpass the fifty thousand dollar plateau went to a series 1899 silver certificate bearing the face denomination of $2 and the back value of $1. Since that time, numerous double denominations have eclipsed that plateau.

The incomparable Frank Levitan collection of United States paper Money, auctioned by Lyn F. Knight in December of 1998, encompassed fourteen different varieties of the double denomination mistake, amidst a host of other incredibly rare notes. The Levitan sale holds the record for the most double denominations publicly offered for sale since the landmark auctions of the Albert A. Grinnell collection more than one-half century before. The probability of a future collector equaling the feat seems infinitesimally small.

The sale of the landmark Taylor Family Collection, conducted by Heritage-Currency Auctions of America, in February of 2005 offered nearly as many, with ten distinct varieties. Every example met or exceeded the pre-sale estimate. The Taylor Family Collection will long be remembered as possessing greater depth, in the field of paper money errors, than any other collection formed.

Still the most astonishing report concerning double denominations involves the American Numismatic Association show in Houston (Texas) during the 1980s. At the convention, Harry E. Jones purchased and sold a dozen pieces of the 1974 series $20 face/$10 back, shortly after their release.

New York paper money dealer, Carl Bombara, relates an interesting story which initially stirred his interest. He heard reports of a series 1996 $100 FRN printed on paper intended for the five dollar denomination. The stock contained the security thread and watermark of the lower denomination. A cursory examination immediately revealed removal of the design of the $5 value via mechanical or chemical methods and a crude photocopy of the $100 denomination. In general commerce, the note would pass testing with a counterfeit-detection pen (designed to verify contents of the paper) but, the ersatz image was woefully inadequate to fool a specialist.

Despite the high price tag on double denominations, dealers who purchase these for inventory typically reap only a modest profit. In the late-1980s, when the error traded in the five thousand dollar range, the sale yielded a ten percent profit. In the current millennium, when double denominations sell for twenty-five to seventy-five thousand dollars, the transaction now nets the dealer closer to five percent.

During my on-camera interviews with NBC reporters (2000) and CNN correspondents (2002), the only error to elicit unabashed excitement from the jaded professionals was the double denomination. Neither tremendously rare nor especially eye-appealing, the double denomination will remain perennially popular...and expensive

TABLE OF DOUBLE DENOMINATIONS

FRACTIONAL CURRENCY

Denominations face / back	Issue	Catalog number (face)
5c/50c	2nd	KL-3229, Fr-1235
---/50c		KL-xxxx-SP, Fr-xxxx-SP (1)
50c/10c		KL-3245-SP, Fr-1314-SP (2)

LARGE SIZE NOTES (EXCEPT NATIONAL CURRENCY)

Denominations face / back	Type	Series	Catalog number (face)
$2 / $1	SC	1899	KL-139, Fr-258
$2 / $1	FRBN	1918	KL-146, Fr-747 (Boston)
			KL-147, Fr-748 (Boston)
			KL-150, Fr-751 (New York)
			KL-155, Fr-756 (Philadelphia)
			KL-164, Fr-765 (Chicago)
$5 / $10	FRN	1914	KL-296, Fr-868 (Chicago)
$20 / $10	FRN	1914	KL-610, Fr-964 (Boston)
			KL-634, Fr-988 (Chicago) (3)

LARGE SIZE NATIONAL CURRENCY

Denominations face / back	Series	Charter	Bank name, City, State
$10 / $20	1865	181	Second National Bank of Springfield, MA
	1195		National Bank of Middlebury, VT
	1882	5225	Bank of Pittsburgh National Assoc., Pittsburgh, PA (4)
		5311	First National Bank, Smithton, PA (4)
		5318	Lowry National Bank, Atlanta, GA (4)
		5760	Old Citizens National Bank of Zanesville, OH (4)
		5771	First National Bank, Barry, IL (4)
		5896	Citizens National Bank, Houghton, MI (4)
		5936	First National Bank, Northport, NY (4)
	1902	414	Second National Bank, Baltimore, MD (4)
		4541	Great Falls National Bank, Great Falls, MT
		6661	First National Bank, Parkers Prairie, MN (4)
		8542	American National Bank, Paris, TX (4)
		10610	National Bank of Lumberton, NC
		11142	Northwestern National Bank, Grand Forks, ND
$20 / $10	1882	860	First National Bank, Washington, NJ (4)
		2524	German National Bank, Cincinnati, OH (4)

Denominations face / back	Series	Charter	Bank name, City, State
		5225	Bank of Pittsburgh National Assoc., Pittsburgh, PA (4)
		5311	First National Bank, Smithton, PA (4)
		5318	Lowry National Bank, Atlanta, GA (4)
		5760	Old Citizens National Bank of Zanesville, OH (4)
		5771	First National Bank, Barry, IL (4)
	1902	414	Second National Bank, Baltimore, MD (4)
		602	Bank of North America, Philadelphia, PA
		6661	First National Bank, Parkers Prairie, MN (4)
		8532	National City Bank, Chicago, IL
		8542	American National Bank, Paris, TX (4)
		11142	Northwestern National Bank, Grand Forks, ND
$50 / $100	1882	2614	First National Bank, Albuquerque, New Mexico Territory (4)
		4251	Aetna National Bank, Kansas City, MO (4)
		4741	Columbia National Bank, Buffalo, NY (4)
$100 / $50	1882	2614	First National Bank, Albuquerque, New Mexico Territory (4)
		4741	Columbia National Bank, Buffalo, NY (4)

SMALL SIZE NOTES

Denominations face / back	Type	Series	Block	Catalog number (face)
$5 / $10	FRN	1934-D	J-D	KL-1788, Fr-1960-J (Kansas City)
$10 / $1	FRN/SC	1950-A	B-D	KL-2100, Fr-2011-B (New York) (5)
$10 / $5	FRN	1928-A	E-A	KL-2002, Fr-2001-E (Richmond) (6)
$20 / $10	FRN	1974	K-B	KL-2509, Fr-2071-K (Dallas) (7)

(1) narrow margin, uniface specimen back with red printing of fifty cent design and bronze surcharge "10" of ten cent denomination
(2) experimental; stamped "SPECIMEN" in purple ink on both sides;contains two semi-lunar punch cancellations; lacking bronze denominationsurcharges both sides
(3) cut sheet of four intact at time of publication of first edition (1994); now dispersed
(4) back design inverted relative to front printing
(5) face design of FRN; back design of SC
(6) twelve notes in Albert A. Grinnell sale (lot 5697A), November 30, 1946; later separated; most demonstrate minor to extensive evidence of prior mounting (especially tightly trimmed margin) along left edge

SERIAL NUMBER CENSUS OF
SMALL SIZE DOUBLE DENOMINATIONS

$5 / $10 FRN 1934-D
J 43180723 A
J 43180743 A
J 43180744 A
J 43180746 A
J 43180748 A
J 43180749 A
J 43180750 A
J 43180814 A
J 43180815 A
J43180815 A
J 43180816 A
J 43180817 A
J 43180819 A
J 43180820 A
J 43180822 A
J 43180823 A
J 43180824 A
J 43180826 A
J 43180827 A
J 43180828 A
J 43180829 A
J 43312744 A
J 43312749 A
J 43312750 A
J 43312751 A
J 43312752 A
J 43312813 A
J 43312817 A
J 43312818 A
J 43312820 A
J 43312821 A
J 43312823 A
J 43312824 A
J 43312825 A
J 43312826 A
J 43312827 A
J 48180749 A
J 543 18017 A

$10 / $1 FRN / SC 1950-A
B 52580340 D
B 52600340 D
B 52620340 D
B 52680340 D
B 52700340 D
B52720340 D
B 52820340 D
B 52860340 D

$10 / $5 FRN 1928-A
E 04672279 A
E 04672280 A
E 04672281 A
E 04742279 A
E 04742280 A
E 04742281 A
E 04742282 A
E 04742284 A

$20 / $10 FRN 1974
K 46318252 B
K 46318253 B
K 46318254 B
K 46338254 B
K 46358252 B
K 46358253 B
K 46438254 B
K 46438255 B
K 46458252 B
K 46458253 B
K 46458254 B
K 46658254 B
K 46678151 B
K 46678252 B
K 46678254 B
K 46696252 B
K 46698252 B
K 46698253 B
K 46698254 B

$10 / $5   FRN   1928-A Double denomination   R-9

Fine: $25,000   EF: $35,000   CU: $45,000

$5 / $10   FRN   1934-D Double denomination   R-9

Fine: $15,000   EF: $25,000   CU: $30,000

$10 / $1	FRN/SC	1950-A Double denomination; error transcends two distinct types of paper money with the face of a Federal Reserve note and back silver of a certificate.	R-9

Fine: $25,000   **EF: $35,000**   **CU: $55,000**

$20 / $10   FRN   1974 Double denomination   R-9

Fine: $20,000   EF: $30,000   CU: $40,000

$5 / $1 FRN   1988-A   Double denomination;   R-9
                                  back design of one dollar
                                  denomination impressed into
                                  heavy ink smear atop correct
                                  five dollar back.

Fine: $10,000   EF: $15,000   CU: $25,000

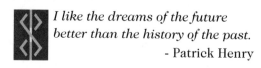

I like the dreams of the future
better than the history of the past.
- Patrick Henry

FAULTY ALIGNMENTS

The faulty alignment error results from an improper relationship between the printed design on one side of the note relative to the other. The currency sheet accepts the printing of one side off-register in comparison to the other side which bears a correctly positioned image.

Faulty alignment errors are correctly centered on one side. This criterion differentiates a faulty alignment mistake from a cutting error. The overprint frequently appears shifted, if the misalignment affects the second print. However, in actuality, the third printing rests in the correct position relative to the edges of the note.

Once the sheet is cut into individual notes, the affected side will have a portion of the adjacent note evident next to the primary note, or at least an abnormally wide margin of blank currency stock. The direction and magnitude of the misalignment-coupled with a particular note's position on the uncut sheet-determines whether the final product will include a segment of the adjacent design or a wide border.

The faulty alignment error is, in common vernacular, an "out of box"

mistake. This refers to a mis-position of the back design beyond the boundaries of the design frame on the front. If uncertain as to the existence or etiology, the easiest method is to hold the note towards a strong light source. Observe the relationship between the face and back designs. If the design border from the back (which is smaller than the face design on all modern United States paper money) falls outside of the rectangular "box" formed by the face design, then a faulty alignment exists. Obviously, the greater the magnitude of misalignment the more spectacular is the visual appearance and consequently the more desirable the piece.

Fractional notes. Several significant examples of the faulty alignment error on fractional currency have traded publicly in recent years. In general, one major example sells annually. A select handful of stunning specimens exhibit one centimeter or more of the adjacent note alongside the primary note. Unlike most types of errors on fractional currency where minor examples are scarce-moderate off-register printings prove readily available, even in high grade.

Large size notes. Except for a few specimens on series 1914 Federal Reserve notes, most notably the five dollar denomination, the spectrum of large size paper money is devoid of major faulty alignment errors. Moderate examples appear on the "Black Eagle" design of the series 1899 one dollar silver certificates and series 1918 Federal Reserve bank notes. Minor varieties surface with some regularity on series 1923 one dollar silver certificates and series 1902 National currency.

Small size notes. Magnificent examples of the faulty alignment error on small size paper money have been infrequently available for decades. Inexplicably, unprecedented numbers of legitimately dramatic specimens became somewhat more plentiful in the mid- to late-1990s, but this abundance was short-lived.

Minor misalignments of the printings are common enough to continue through circulation, even among those astute enough to recognize the mistake. As a general guide to value, unless the error is immediately apparent, the note merits no premium. In fact, even those notes that show the design border from the adjacent note carry only a modest premium when in crisp uncirculated condition...and essentially zero premium when on circulated, high denomination pieces.

Locating minor to moderate off-register printings on small size notes presents little challenge. Besides the commonly available Federal Reserve notes (FRN) and silver certificates (SC), the error also exists, in limited numbers, on gold certificates, national currency, United States notes, and Federal Reserve bank notes. However, truly spectacular varieties exist only on FRN and SC; more notably the former.

Insights and Incidents. Faulty alignment errors have come into greater favor among collectors, due to the increase in the availability of truly stunning specimens. The observation "...dramatic examples do not capture prices commensurate with their true rarity." asserted in the first edition no longer routinely holds true. In fact, the value of major misalignments has increased nearly tenfold, outperforming many other categories of paper money errors.

Minor faulty alignments continue to be shunned by dealers and collectors alike. In the current marketplace, one magnificent example, at twenty times the cost-remains preferable to ten lesser pieces at one-half of the price. Eye-appeal means everything.

There exists a paucity of dramatic examples on the redesigned paper money which began with the series of 1996 $100 denomination. An unknown variable within the Bureau of Engraving and Printing has changed, either production of faulty alignment errors has fallen to near-zero or the inspection technology has increased to near perfect as so few are encountered. A collector, in the enviable position of seeing a significant example, would do well to acquire it.

EXAMPLES OF THE ERROR

MINOR

MODERATE

MAJOR

$1   FRN   1974   Faulty alignment; major   R-6
      Fine: $500   EF: $1500   CU: $2500

$1   FRN   1969-B   Faulty alignment; moderate   R-4
      Fine: $150   EF: $350   CU: $650

$1   FRN   1988-A   Faulty alignment; minor   R-2
      Fine: $25   EF: $75   CU: $150

$1	FRN	1988-A	Faulty alignment; major	R-6

Fine: $250   **EF: $750**   **CU: $1500**

$1	FRN	1988-A	Faulty alignment; major	R-6

Fine: $250   **EF: $750**   **CU: $1500**

$1	FRN	1995	Faulty alignment; major	R-6

Fine: $1000   **EF: $2500**   **CU: $4500**

$1   FRN   1995   Faulty alignment; major   R-6
        Fine: **$1500**   EF: **$4500**   CU: **$8500**

$1   FRN   1995   Faulty alignment; major   R-6
        Fine: **$500**   EF: **$1250**   CU: **$2500**

$2   USN   1953   Faulty alignment; minor
        Fine: **$150**   EF: **$350**   CU: **$500**

$2	USN	1953-A	Faulty alignment; minor	
	Fine: $50		**EF: $150**	**CU: $250**

$2	FRN	1976	Faulty alignment; minor mirror image of above seal	R-3
	Fine: $50		**EF: $150**	**CU: $250**

$2	FRN	1976	Faulty alignment; minor	R-3
	Fine: $25		**EF: $75**	**CU: $150**

| $5 | FRN | 1977-A | Faulty alignment; minor | R-2 |

Fine: $25   **EF: $35**   **CU: $50**

| $5 | FRN | 1988-A | Faulty alignment; major | R-6 |

this note—and note below—from same
sheet, the difference in appearance
due to different positions on sheet

Fine: $750   **EF: $1500**   **CU: $2500**

| $5 | FRN | 1988-A | Faulty alignment; major | R-6 |

refer to comments above

Fine: $750   **EF: $1500**   **CU: $2500**

| $10 | FRN | 1950 | Faulty alignment; minor | R-2 |

Fine: $25   **EF: $50**   **CU: $100**

| $10 | FRN | 1950-A | Faulty alignment; major | R-6 |

Fine: $250   **EF: $500**   **CU: $1000**

| $10 | FRN | 1985 | Faulty alignment; major | R-6 |

Fine: $750   **EF: $1500**   **CU: $2500**

$10	FRN	1988-A	Faulty alignment; minor	R-2
	Fine: $25		EF: $50	CU: $100

$10	FRN	1988-A	Faulty alignment; major	R-6
	Fine: $500		EF: $1250	CU: $2500

$10	FRN	1988-A	Faulty alignment; major	R-6
	Fine: $750		EF: $1500	CU: $2500

$10	FRN	1990	Faulty alignment; moderate	R-4

Fine: $75   **EF: $150**   **CU: $250**

$20	FRN	1981	Faulty alignment; moderate	R-4

Fine: $150   **EF: $350**   **CU: $750**

$20	FRN	1985	Faulty alignment; moderate	R-4

Fine: $100   **EF: $200**   **CU: $350**

$20	FRN	1988-A	Faulty alignment; minor	R-2

Fine: $35   **EF: $50**   **CU: $100**

$10	FRN	1988-A	Faulty alignment; major	R-6

Fine: $1500   **EF: $3500**   **CU: $6500**

$10	FRN	1988-A	Faulty alignment; major	R-6

Fine: $2000   **EF: $5000**   **CU: $9500**

$20	FRN	1996	Faulty alignment; moderate		R-4
	Fine: $50		**EF: $150**	**CU: $350**	

$20	FRN	1996	Faulty alignment; minor		R-2
	Fine: $50		**EF: $150**	**CU: $200**	

$50	FRN	1981	Faulty alignment; major		R-6
			portions of four different notes show		
	Fine: $500		**EF: $1000**	**CU: $1500**	

$50	FRN	1985	Faulty alignment; major	R-6
	Fine: $1500		EF: $2500	CU: $4500

$50	FRN	1996	Faulty alignment; minor	R-2
	Fine: $100		EF: $150	CU: $250

$100	FRN	1996	Faulty alignment; major	R-6
	Fine: $1000		EF: $3000	CU: $4500

$100   FRN   1996   Faulty alignment; minor   R-2
        Fine: $125   EF: $150   CU: $200

$100   FRN   1996   Faulty alignment; minor   R-2
        Fine: $150   EF: $250   CU: $350

$100   FRN   1996   Faulty alignment; minor   R-6
        Fine: $125   EF: $150   CU: $200

As I grow to understand life less and less,
I learn to love it more and more.

- Jules Renard

INK SMEARS

Ink smears result from inadequately cleaned printing plates. The amount of residual ink left on the surface of the plate determines the size and shape of the smear, which many range from a fine line or small spot to a broad band covering the entire face or back design. The extra ink either obliterates a portion of the intended design or covers areas normally left blank. The value or premium commanded by an ink smear relates directly to the size of the excess ink.

Under proper operating conditions, the ink fountain in the press machinery "charges" or covers the entire thirty-two subject printing plate, allowing some ink to fill the engraved intaglio design, with the surplus ink remaining on the surface. The plate then encounters a reciprocating mechanical wiper that removes the surface ink without disturbing the fluid resting in the incuse recesses forming the design. After a printing pass, wherein the plate makes contact with an uncut sheet of currency stock, the plate receives an application of a cleaning or solvent solution. The solvent serves to dilute the remaining ink, facilitating the cleaning process. The plate then encounters another mechanical wiper that removes the

diluted ink, before being flooded or charged for the next printing run.

A performance failure within the series of reciprocating wipers or the protracted use of dirty wiper rolls allows the ink to remain on the plate and causes the familiar ink smear error.

In contrast to ink smears affecting the first or second printings, whose cause is outlined above, smears on the overprint typically occur due to an application of excess ink to the heads printing the serial numbers or seals. Ink s mears involving the overprint, arise far less frequently than those on the first or second print. Alternatively, impatient press operators at the Bureau of Engraving and Printing (BEP) often grab the top sheet in a stack causing smearing or smudging of the overprint.

The designation "solvent smear" is a misnomer. It belies the true cause, as the error actually represents heavily diluted ink-not solvent-which smears. The mistake occurs when an excessive amount of the solvent solution reaches the printing plate. Unless the reciprocal wipers extract the excess, the residual solvent dilutes the consistency of the fresh layer of ink. The watery ink produces a blurry, hazy, and indistinct image on the printed design.

Ink smears lend themselves to fakery more readily than other types of errors, by the application of additional ink outside of the BEP. Nonetheless, with minimal experience, it becomes fairly simple to distinguish genuine smears by their texture. A government-manufactured error possesses a certain "look and feel" that seems virtually impossible to duplicate after the note reaches circulation.

Fractional notes. Since the publication of the first edition, the author has examined six or seven pieces of fractional currency bearing seemingly genuine characteristics of ink smears. In each case, the excess ink assumed an ovoid or blotch configuration, rather than a linear pattern common on modern small size paper money. All specimens, except one, came from the first issue (five cent and ten cent denominations); the other a twenty-five cent note from the third issue. These Civil War-era paper substitutes for coinage were surface printed or lithographed.

Large size notes. Large size paper money began with the series 1861 Demand Notes; they terminated with the series of 1923 silver certificates and United States notes. Despite the long time frame, ink smears appear rather infrequently on large size notes. Additionally, the smears tend to be proportionately smaller than those found on the reduced size currency. Among those documented, most are one dollar notes from the

series of 1899 and 1923. A major ink smear on a piece of large size currency would be a newsworthy discovery.

Small size notes. Ink smears represent the most common collectible small size paper money error; more escape the visual and electronic inspections at the BEP than any other mistake. Although minor smears appear fairly regularly (a mean average of one identifiable ink smear per one thousand notes searched), massive smears covering 25% or more of one side remain extremely elusive. Major ink smears can be confirmed on every class of small size notes except national currency, Federal Reserve bank notes, and gold certificates.

Solvent smears-which on the average-affect a larger surface area than an ink smear are restricted to Federal Reserve notes and silver certificates.

The latest variety of ink smear—or at least over inking—are a small group of "test" notes intentionally printed, but slated to be destroyed. At the start of each printing shift, plates are completely flooded with excess ink to test the press. The ink covers the entire printing plate, with the exception of rectangular areas on the surface of the plate where no intaglio recesses exist to hold the ink. After testing the press, the sheet is to be removed and destroyed. About six to eight examples are known affecting the backs of $1 denomination. Three examples are known to affect the face, including one with a replacement serial number.

Insights and Incidents. Ink smears, the most plentiful BEP mistake to escape, and their cousins, the solvent smears, generally are ignored. Unfortunately, even significant to spectacular examples generate little interest when offered for sale. The single exception is ink smears on two dollar FRNs. These seem to trade at prices above their actual scarcity. Although historically two dollar errors have proven challenging to locate, literally hundreds of errors (of varying magnitudes and types) surfaced between 1993-1995 as banks cleared series 1976 deuces from their vaults to accept the newly-printed series 1995. There was a much smaller flood of errors, as banks evacuated the series 1995 to make room for the series 2003 and 2003-A notes.

Internet auction sites are awash with spurious errors. Among those seen most often (aside from pseudo-cutting errors and extraneous printings applied outside of the BEP) are faked ink smears. Unfortunately, the uninformed and greedy fall victim to these scams, as most listings end with a completed sale. Today's "bargain" becomes tomorrow's disappointment, when the truth is uncovered. The astute collector will judiciously pursue acquiring superb specimens of the ink and solvent smear errors, at favorable prices, in about uncirculated or better condition. As with any error, being prepared to "stretch" to acquire an exceptional example generally proves to be a wise decision as time passes.

EXAMPLES OF THE ERROR

MINOR

MODERATE

MAJOR

| $1 | FRN | 1995 | Solvent smear | R-3 |
| | Fine: $50 | | EF: $150 | CU: $350 |

| $1 | FRN | 1995 | Ink smear; major flooded pattern to test plate | R-4 |
| | Fine: $150 | | EF: $350 | CU: $750 |

| $1 | FRN | 1999 | Ink smear; minor | R-1 |
| | Fine: $15 | | EF: $25 | CU: $50 |

$2   FRN   1976   Ink smear; minor   R-2

Fine: $25   **EF: $50**   **CU: $75**

$2   FRN   1976   Ink smear; major   R-5

Fine: $250   **EF: $500**   **CU: $750**

$2   FRN   1976   Solvent smear   R-4

Fine: $50   **EF: $100**   **CU: $200**

$2   FRN   1976   Ink smear; major   R-5
      Fine: $100   EF: $250   CU: $500

$5   FRN   1977   Ink smear; major   R-4
      Fine: $75   EF: $100   CU: $150

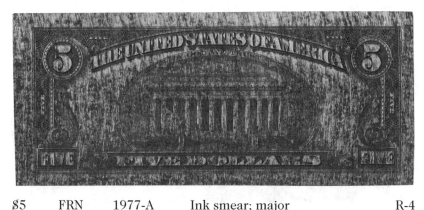

$5   FRN   1977-A   Ink smear; major   R-4
                       note wiper pattern
      Fine: $150   EF: $300   CU: $500

| $5 | FRN | 1988-A | Ink smear; minor | R-1 |
| Fine: $25 | | EF: $50 | | CU: $75 |

| $10 | FRN | 1969-C | Ink smear; moderate | R-2 |
| Fine: $25 | | EF: $50 | | CU: $75 |

| $10 | FRN | 1977-A | Ink smear; major | R-4 |
| Fine: $150 | | EF: $250 | | CU: $450 |

$20	FRN	1988-A	Ink smear; major resembles matte pattern offset	R-4

Fine: $150   **EF: $250**   **CU: $450**

$50	FRN	1977	Ink smear; major	R-4

Fine: $75   **EF: $150**   **CU: $250**

Exert your talents, and distinguish yourself, and don't think of retiring from the world, until the world will be sorry that you retire.

- Samuel Johnson

INSUFFICIENT INKINGS

The insufficient inking error develops when the ink fountain fails to fully charge or fill the printing plate with ink. The ink fountain stores the ink alongside the press. When the reservoir runs low, pressure weakens, or a partial obstruction in the supply tube occurs, inadequate amounts of ink flood the intaglio design in the plate. The net result is a printed image which is faint or incomplete.

The insufficient inking may affect all or part of the design, depending upon the area affected on the printing plate. Typically, the error involves a significant portion of, if not the entire, design. However, isolated segments of insufficient ink are not uncommon. Predictably, the larger the insufficiently inked area the greater the premium.

Most insufficient inking mistakes appear on the first or second printing. The overprint is occasionally affected. The typical presentation of insufficient ink on the third print involves a single digit in the serial number which in whole or part is absent. Less commonly, the entire green or black elements of the bi-color overprint are missing.

Numerous anti-counterfeiting devices were incorporated into United States paper money commencing with the series 1990. The heightened measures included micro printing surrounding the portrait oval, use of an embedded polymer security thread, and utilization of magnetic ink for portions of the face printing, among other techniques. Implementation of magnetic ink gave rise to a new breed of insufficient inking errors, as alternate fountains were filled with magnetic and nonmagnetic ink. The overall pattern resembles a checkerboard. Most examples of the missing magnetic ink begin at the left end of the face, in the upper and lower corners; sometimes extending, in sections, across the entire front. The etiology of the segmental missing magnetic ink is identical to insufficient inking errors.

Fractional notes. The two alleged insufficient inking errors on fractional currency examined by the author are in circulated condition. As such, it was impossible to unhesitatingly declare them genuine; likewise, inadequate proof existed to deem them alterations. Drawing a definite conclusion, from such tenuous evidence, would have been irresponsible.

Large size notes. Examples of the insufficient inking error on large size paper money appear infrequently. Several notes-most notably from the series 1923 one dollar silver certificates-show inadequate ink applied to the digit(s) within the serial number. One example from the series 1917 one dollar United States notes, demonstrates insufficient ink on the entire overprint; the note grades crisp uncirculated, remains deeply embossed, and appears utterly unmolested. Many heavily circulated large size notes lack the overprint; all suggest a prior washing and/or exposure to chemical vapors. Their authenticity is doubted by most authorities.

A literal smattering of large size notes demonstrates irregular areas of insufficient ink. Caution must be exercised when evaluating these, as alterations (either accidental or deliberate) outnumber genuine pieces.

There are no verified examples of an entire back or face printed from inadequately inked plates.

Small size notes. The insufficient inking error is generally elusive on notes manufactured prior to the series 1963. The Giori presses, which the Bureau of Engraving and Printing still employs, were introduced slowly with the series of 1963. The Giori presses replaced the sheet-fed rotary and flatbed presses. Along with greatly expanded production capabilities, errors of previously limited occurrence began to surface...including examples of the insufficient inking error. Despite technological advances in subsequent presses, notes with inadequate ink on the design continue to escape the BEP.

Staggering quantities of one dollar series 1988 Federal Reserve notes-and to a lesser extent series of 1988-A-were printed with defective black ink for the second printing. The finished notes visually appeared perfect through the final inspection phases at the BEP. Ultimately, the ink flaked off while the notes passed through circulation! Representatives from the BEP refused to acknowledge changes in the ink formulation or provide a technical explanation as to the cause. These error notes are extremely common and command essentially no premium.

Perhaps the most intriguing insufficient ink errors affects and uncut sheet of series 1995 $2 notes. The upper twenty-four notes (four columns wide by six notes deep) are lacking the green Treasury seals which then progressively return to normal. The sheet is from the F-E block.

Notes with insufficient inking of the face and back design should exist with equal frequency. However, fewer examples are encountered with poor inking on the face. Those with a faint impression of either the black or green portions of the third printing are even less available. A few isolated specimens of insufficient inking exist on the later series of silver certificates. Two dollar and five dollar United States notes rarely contain insufficient inking; when the error appears it involves only a portion of the design. There are no documented examples of the error involving either the entire face or back printing on national currency, Federal Reserve bank notes, or gold certificates. Two pieces of 1929 national currency with alleged insufficient ink have been examined; both were altered.

Insights and Incidents. Between the releases of the first two editions, two significant "hoards" of insufficient inking errors escaped the BEP. A group of nearly one hundred fifty sequential

$20 series 1993 FRNs from the New York district surfaced at the Florida United Numismatists (FUN) convention in Orlando in 1997. The mistake involved varying degrees of inadequate ink on the back, typically affecting the left end. The other large quantity of insufficient inking errors released were an estimated six hundred pieces (four original consecutive packs verified by the author) of series 1995 $5 notes from the Richmond district. The light to absent ink bothered the green serial numbers and Treasury seal. Most examples showed a single digit-in the seventh or eighth position-lightly but, legibly inked. The remainder of the green portion of the overprint was entirely missing. Prices fluctuated wildly with the notes trading wholesale at fifty to one hundred twenty-five dollars. All packs were initially distributed by Brink's from a shipment of new money. Two or three packs surfaced in St. Louis; another two hundred notes came out in the San Francisco bay area. Due to the extensive marketing of both the series 1993 $20 and the series 1995 $5 FRNs, interest in insufficient inking errors has increased slightly.

A facet of insufficient ink errors garnering escalating attention and prices are notes missing large portions of the second or face print. Such pieces demonstrate the green and black portions of the overprint against a stark white background. This makes for thrilling viewing. At the risk of redundancy, "sex appeal" drives the error market now more than ever.

One of the anti-counterfeiting methods initiated on the redesigned small size paper money, which began with series 1996 $100 denomination, was the use of a color shift ink. The color shift ink appears in the lower right corner of the face. It changes from black to green as the note moves from a vertical to horizontal position. The color shift ink is applied over a waffle pattern constructing the numerals equal to the denomination. Large quantities of insufficient to entirely absent color shift ink entered the marketplace. Collectors, in general, were unimpressed. Overall, the notes sold poorly. Eventually, at least two dealers spent the examples remaining in their inventories at face value!

A cursory search of the more popular internet auction sites uncovers altered notes being represented as genuine BEP errors on a daily basis. The two types of errors most frequently counterfeited are additional printings (multiple printings and offsets) and missing printings (insufficient or absent inkings). In many instances, the seller--who often creates these himself--doesn't fully understand the printing stages. Not too uncommonly, an alteration advertised as a genuine insufficient inking might have portions of two different printings affected; for example, the "error" might show light ink on the portrait and serial number.

Quite bluntly, establishing the authenticity of an insufficient inking error generally takes mere seconds--providing the examiner has adequate experience. Unfortunately, very few of the graders for the third-party services have in-depth knowledge of the error field. Bogus insufficient inking mistakes sometimes end up being certified as genuine and encapsulated. Don't allow a plastic entombment to be the ultimate assurance of authenticity.

EXAMPLES OF THE ERROR

MINOR

MODERATE

MAJOR

$1	FRN	19xx	Insufficient ink; face	R-4
	Fine: $250		EF: $500	CU: $850

$1	FRN	1969-B	Insufficient ink; back	R-3
	Fine: $125		EF: $250	CU: $500

$1	FRN	1969-C	Insufficient ink; face	R-4
	Fine: $100		EF: $250	CU: $500

$1	FRN	1977-A	Insufficient ink; overprint	R-4

Fine: $50   EF: **$100**   CU: **$250**

$1	FRN	1985	Insufficient ink; front improper batting caused inadequate application of ink	R-4

Fine: $125   EF: **$250**   CU: **$350**

$1	FRN	2003-A	Insufficient ink; back	R-3

Fine: $100   EF: **$200**   CU: **$300**

$2	FRN	1976	Insufficient ink; single digit	R-3
Fine: $25		**EF: $50**		**CU: $75**

$2	FRN	1976	Insufficient ink; back	R-4
Fine: $250		**EF: $500**		**CU: $1000**

$5	FRN	19xx	Insufficient ink; face	R-4
Fine: $150		**EF: $350**		**CU: $650**

$5	FRN	19xx	Insufficient ink; face	R-5

Fine: $350   EF: $750   CU: $1250

$5	FRN	1977	Insufficient ink; front	R-4

Fine: $100   EF: $200   CU: $350

$5	FRN	1995	Insufficient ink; overprint	R-4

Fine: $50   EF: $100   CU: $250

$10	FRN	1981	Insufficient ink; back		R-3
	Fine: $50		EF: $100	CU: $200	

$20	FRN	19xx	Insufficient ink; face		R-4
	Fine: $200		EF: $400	CU: $650	

$20	FRN	1974	Insufficient ink; back		R-3
	Fine: $100		EF: $200	CU: $300	

$20	FRN	1977	Insufficient ink; face	R-4
	Fine: $200		EF: $400	CU: $650

$20	FRN	1993	Insufficient ink; back	R-3
	Fine: $50		EF: $75	CU: $100

$50	FRN	1977	Insufficient ink; back	R-3
	Fine: $150		EF: $350	CU: $650

$50	FRN	1985	Insufficient ink; face	R-4
	Fine: $300		**EF: $650**	**CU: $1250**

$100	FRN	1985	Insufficient ink; back	R-3
	Fine: $200		**EF: $350**	**CU: $750**

$100	FRN	1985	Insufficient ink; back	R-3
	Fine: $150		**EF: $250**	**CU: $500**

$100	FRN	1996	Insufficient ink; back	R-3
	Fine: $150		**EF: $250**	**CU: $350**

$100	FRN	1996	Insufficient ink; back	R-3
	Fine: $125		**EF: $175**	**CU: $250**

*Never mistake knowledge for wisdom.
One helps you make a living,
the other helps you make a life.*

- Sandara Carey

INVERTED BACKS

In actuality, the so-called "inverted back" error is an inverted face. Although the verso appears upside down when viewing both sides of the note from the front-as in turning a page in a book-the traditional designation "inverted back" contradicts the printing sequence. At the Bureau of Engraving and Printing, the back of the note accepts the first printing operation and rightfully should serve as the reference to judge the alignment of subsequent printings.

The inverted back error arises when a stack of currency sheets, after receiving the first (or back) printing, rotates 180 degrees and enters the presses upside down for the face and overprinting stages. Considering: [1] that the uncut sheets are physically moved between printings-therefore subject to potentially having the ends transposed and [2] when viewed independently, each side of the completed paper money appears perfect unto itself, one can readily appreciate the probability for manufacture and release of the inverted back. This type of mistake exists on virtually every category of United States paper money from colonial currency through fractional currency and military payment certificates to modern size Federal Reserve notes.

Fractional notes. The inverted positioning of the face design occurs on every denomination of fractional currency. Examples exist on nearly fifty percent of the major types within this class of paper money. The five cent de-

nomination of the first issue, authorized by the Act of March 3, 1863, (specifically Fr-1230), provides the most abundant specimens. An uncut twenty subject sheet bearing inverted backs appeared at auction in 1980, more than one century after its accidental manufacture. In uncirculated condition, inverted backs remain relatively more available on the shin-plaster notes than on either large or small size paper money.

Large size notes. As opposed to most errors, inverted backs exist in relatively greater supply on large size currency than on modern paper money. This mistake involves large size United States notes, silver certificates, Federal Reserve notes, treasury notes, national currency, gold certificates, and Federal Reserve bank notes; none of the seven denominations between $1 and $100 is exempt. Locating a high-grade piece presents a formidable challenge, as most circulated unnoticed. The series of 1899 $1 silver certificates (Fr-233) yielded the most examples. Slightly more than one dozen large size star or replacement notes with inverted backs are known; each represents a legitimate rarity.

Small size notes. The collector seeking an example of the inverted back error must rely upon the series of 1928 $1 silver certificates and the series of 1928 and 1934 $5 and $10 Federal Reserve notes. The error affects countless blocks among the silver certificates and numerous districts on the Federal Reserve notes.

Unquestionably, the list of currently reported blocks is incomplete. The inverts known represent all states of preservation, from about good to gem crisp uncirculated, although predictably they favor the circulated grades. The error exists on all denominations from $1 through $100. When both the front and back are correctly centered—which typifies the error prior to the series of 1981-A—the designation of a Type I inverted back is applied. However, changes within the BEP began with the series of 1981-A included trimming the top selvedge of the sheet before the second printing. Such inverted backs show a major misalignment on the verso, demonstrating either a broad white margin or a portion of the adjacent note. Such mistakes are characterized as Type II.

Insights and Incidents. The inverted back error-while always moderately popular-receives more attention now than at any time in the past. Two logical explanations exist for this occurrence: [1] collectors are finally beginning to recognize the genuine scarcity of the error on small size notes, especially in extremely fine or better and [2] unlike other types of mistakes, the Bureau of Engraving and Printing has proven stingy in the release of inverted backs during the past sixty years. While a few trickle out occasionally on modern FRNs, the supply has been woefully inadequate.

Prices on inverted backs-like all United States paper money errors-have escalated dramatically since the publication of the last edition. "Common" inverted backs (series of 1899 $1 SC, series of 1928 and 1934 $5 and $10 FRNs, and series of 1928 $1 SC), in very good to very fine, often garner prices greater than their scarcity might dictate. In contradistinction, genuinely scarce pieces frequently sell at bargain levels, despite keen competition among bidders. Retail sales of inverted backs on FC remain sluggish. Nonetheless, Currency Auction of America's (CAA) sale of the Milton Friedberg collection placed unprecedented numbers of the errors into the hands of collectors, many at very strong levels.

Nearly ten years ago, I enjoyed the privilege of offering for sale the largest collection of inverted backs ever formed. The incomparable achievement took twenty years of painstaking dedication. The amazing assemblage, encompassing nearly 300 notes, including many unique varieties in both large and small size It dwarfed the efforts of Albert A. Grinnell and other private collectors and the Smithsonian Institution and other public holdings. A portion of the collection was sold via private treaty; CAA auctioned the remainder in January, 2000. Due to the enormity of the offering, relatively "common" notes in circulated grades sold well-below market value. High grade notes brought prices commensurate with their scarcity. The unique-and extremely rare inverted backs, particularly those in heavily circulated conditions, sold far below what their rarity deserved.

Since 2004 or 2005, the inverted backs under the greatest collector pressure (and bringing the highest prices at auction) are those in high grade, most especially large size notes in crisp uncirculated condition. Even "common" designs, in uncommon condition, will fetch prices beyond the most optimistic of expectations. In a sense, these examples are treated as non-error type notes. Not only does it appear that this trend will continue, but it seems that third-party graded and encapsulated pieces will lead the way.

TABLE OF INVERTED BACKS

FRACTIONAL CURRENCY

Denomination	Issue	Catalog number
3c	3rd	KL-3252, Fr-1226
		KL-3253, Fr-1227
5c	1st	KL-3209, Fr-1228
		KL-3210, Fr-1229
		KL-3211, Fr-1230 (1)
		KL-3212, Fr-1231
	2nd	KL-3226, Fr-1232
		KL-3227, Fr-1233
	3rd	KL-3256, Fr-1238
		KL-3257, Fr-1239
10c	1st	KL-3214, Fr-1241
		KL-3215, Fr-1242
		KL-3216, Fr-1243
	2nd	KL-3230, Fr-1244
		KL-3232, Fr-1246
	3rd	KL 3264, Fr-1256
25c	1st	KL-3218, Fr-1280
		KL-3219, Fr-1281
		KL-3220, Fr-1282
	2nd	KL-3239, Fr-1286
	3rd	KL-3268, Fr-1294
		KL-3270, Fr-1296
50c	1st	KL-3221, Fr-1310
		KL-3222, Fr-1311
		KL-3223, Fr-1312
		KL-3224, Fr-1313
	2nd	KL-3245, Fr-1316
		KL-3246, Fr-1317
		KL-3247, Fr-1318
		KL-3249, Fr-1321
		KL-3250, Fr-1322
	3rd	KL-3283, Fr-1331
		KL-3284, Fr-1332
		KL-3285, Fr-1333
		KL-3286, Fr-1334
		KL-3290, Fr-1338
		KL-3291, Fr-1339
		KL-3309, Fr-1357
		KL-3317, Fr-1365
		KL-3322, Fr-1370

LARGE SIZE NOTES (EXCEPT NATIONAL CURRENCY)

Denomination	Type	Series	Catalog number
$1	TN	1890	KL-56, Fr-348
			KL-57, Fr-349
		1891	KL-58, Fr-350
			KL-59, Fr-351
			KL-60, Fr-352
	SC	1886	KL-29, Fr-215
			KL-31, Fr-217
		1899	KL-40, Fr-226
			KL-41, Fr-226a
			KL-42, Fr-227
			KL-43, F-228
			KL-44, Fr-229
			KL-45, Fr-230
			KL-45*, Fr-230-* (2)
			KL-47, Fr-232
			KL-47*, Fr-232-*(2)
			KL-48, Fr-233 (3)
			KL-48*, Fr-233-*(2)
			KL-49, Fr-234 (4)
			KL-49*, Fr-234-*(2)
			KL-50, Fr-235
			KL-51, Fr-236
		1923	KL-52, Fr-237
			KL-52*, Fr-237-* (2)
			KL-53, Fr-238
	USN	1917	KL-23, Fr-36
			KL-24, Fr-37
			KL-26, Fr-38
			KL-27, Fr-39
		1923	KL-28, Fr-40
	FRBN	1918	KL-65, Fr-712 (New York)
			KL-70, Fr-717 (Philadelphia)
			KL-71, Fr-718 (Cleveland)
			KL-78, Fr-725 (Atlanta)
			KL-83, Fr-730 (St. Louis)
			KL-90, Fr-737 (Kansas City)
			KL-97, Fr-744 (San Francisco)
$2	SC	1886	KL-123 Fr-242
		1899	KL-130, Fr-249
			KL-132, Fr-251
			KL-134, Fr-253
			KL-136, Fr-255
			KL-137, Fr-256
			KL-139, Fr-258

Denomination	Type	Series	Catalog number
	USN	1880	KL-110, Fr-50
		1917	KL-117, Fr-57
			KL-117*, Fr-57-* (2)
			KL-118, Fr-58
			KL-120, Fr-60, Fr-120-* (2)
	FRBN	1918	KL-150, Fr-751 (New York)
			KL-159, Fr-760 (Richmond)
			KL-166, Fr-767 (Chicago)
$5	SC	1891	KL-237, Fr-267
		1896	KL-240, Fr-270
		1899	KL-241, Fr-271
			KL-242, Fr-272
			KL-243, Fr-273
			KL-244*, Fr-274-*(2)
			KL-245, Fr-275
			KL-247, Fr-277
			KL-250, Fr-280
	USN	1880	KL-207, Fr-77 (5)
		1907	KL-215, Fr-85
			KL-217, Fr-87
			KL-221, Fr-91
	FRN	1914	KL-275, Fr-847 (Boston)
			KL-276, Fr-848 (New York)
			KL-277, Fr-849 (New York)
			KL-280, Fr-852 (Philadelphia)
			KL-298, Fr-870 (Chicago)
			KL-309, Fr-881 (Kansas City)
			KL-316, Fr-888 (San Francisco)
$10	SC	1908	KL-427, Fr-302
	USN	1901	KL-380, Fr-114
			KL-388, Fr-122
	FRN	1914	KL-444, Fr-893 (New York)
			KL-457, Fr-906 (Boston)
			KL-469, Fr-918 (Cleveland)
			KL-495, Fr-944 (Dallas)
	GC	1922	KL-442, Fr-1173
$20	SC	1891	KL-591, Fr-321
			KL-592, Fr-322
	FRN	1914	KL-604, Fr-958 (Chicago; red seal)
			KL-634, Fr-988 (Chicago)
			KL-637, Fr-991 (Chicago)
	GC	1906	KL-562*, Fr-1185-*(2)
		1922	KL-564, Fr-1187
$50	GC	1922	KL-705, Fr-1200
$100	FRN	1914	KL-871, Fr-1098 (Cleveland)

LARGE SIZE NATIONAL CURRENCY

Denomination	Series	Charter	Bank name, City, State
$5	1882	5760	Old Citizens Nat'l Bank, Zanesville, OH
	1902	3600	Commercial Nat'l Bank, Shreveport, LA
$10	1882	5225	Bank of Pittsburgh National Association, Pittsburgh, PA
		5311	First National Bank, Smithton, PA
		5318	Lowry National Bank, Atlanta, GA
		5760	Old Citizens Nat'l Bank, Zanesville, OH
		5771	First National Bank, Barry, IL
		5896	Citizens National Bank, Houghton, MI
		5936	First National Bank, Northport, NY
	1902		414 Second National Bank, Baltimore, MD
		6661	First Nat'l Bank, Parkers Prairie, MN
		8542	American National Bank, Paris, TX

SMALL SIZE NOTES (EXCEPT NATIONAL CURRENCY)

Denomination	Type	Series	Block	Catalog number
$1	SC	1928	A-A	KL-1445, Fr-1600
			C-A	
			E-A	
			F-A	
		1928-A	*-A	KL-1446*, Fr-1601-* (2)
			G-A	KL-1446, Fr-1601
			I-A	
			L-A	
			N-A (6)	
			R-A	
			S-A	
			T-A	
			U-A	
			X-A	
			Y-A	
			Z-A	
		1928-B	E-B	KL-1447, Fr-1602
			F-B	
			G-B	
			H-B	
			I-B	
		1934	*-A	KL-1451*, Fr-1606-* (2)
			A-A	KL-1451, Fr-1606
			B-A	
			C-A	

Denomination	Type	Series	Block	Catalog number
			D-A	
			E-A	
			F-A	
			G-A	
		1935	*-A	KL-1452*, Fr-1607-* (2)
			A-A	KL-1452, Fr-1607
			B-A	
			J-A	
			L-A	
		1935-A	P-A	KL-1453, Fr-1608
			R-A	
			S-A	
			T-A	
			U-A	
			D-B	
			H-B	
			M-B	
			W-B	
			D-C	
			G-C	
			K-C	
			R-C	
			V-C	
		1935-B	H-D	KL-1454, Fr-1609
		1935-C	*-B	KL-1455*, Fr-1610-* (2)
		1935-E	*-D	KL-1457*, Fr-1614-* (2)
			*-E	
			X-G	KL-1457, Fr-1614
			B-H	
			G-H	
	FRN	1974	L-F	KL-1584, Fr-1908 (SanFrancis)(7)
		1985	A-E	KL-3700, Fr-1913 (Boston) (10)
		1995	D-C	KL-4087, Fr-1921(Cleveland)(10)
			F-G	KL-4089, Fr-1921 (Atlanta) (10)
		2003-A	B-*	KL-, Fr-1930 (New York) (2), (10)
$2	USN	1928	A-A	KL-1613, Fr-1501
		1928-C	B-A	KL-1616, Fr-1504
			C-A	
			E-A	
			F-A	
		1928-D	C-A	KL-1617, Fr-1505
			D-A	
		1928-G	B-A	KL-1620, Fr-1508

Denomination	Type	Series	Block	Catalog number
$5	FRBN	1929	G-A	KL-1665, Fr-1850 (Chicago)
	USN	1928	A-A	KL-1639, Fr-1525
			B-A	
			C-A	
		1928-B	D-A	KL-1641, Fr-1527
		1928-E	H-A	KL-1644, Fr-1530
	SC	1934	B-A	KL-1651, Fr-1650
			C-A	
			D-A	
			E-A	
	FRN	1928	A-A	KL-1671, Fr-1950 (Boston)
			C-A	KL-1673, (Philadelphia)
			D-*	KL-1674*, (Cleveland) (2)
			D-A	KL-1674, (Cleveland)
			E-A	KL-1675, (Richmond)
			G-A	KL-1677, (Chicago)
			K-*	KL-1681*, (Dallas) (2)
			K-A	KL-1681, (Dallas)
			L-A	KL-1682, (San Francisco)
		1928-A	A-A	KL-1683, Fr-1951 (Boston)
			B-A	KL-1684, (New York)
			D-A	(KL-1686, Cleveland)
			E-A	(KL-1687, Richmond)
			F-A	KL-1688, (Atlanta)
			G-A	KL-1689, (Chicago)
			H-A	KL-1690, (St. Louis)
		1928-B	A-A	KL-1695, Fr-1952 (Boston)
			D-A	KL-1698, (Cleveland)
		1934	B-A	KL-1732, Fr-1955 (New York)
			D-A	KL-1734, (Cleveland)
			J-A	KL-1740, (Kansas City)
			K-A	KL-1741, (Dallas)
		1934-A	B-*	KL-1744*, Fr-1956-* (New York) (2)
			B-A	KL-1744, Fr-1956 (New York)
		1950	A-A	KL-1791, Fr-1961 (Boston)
		1995	F-B	KL-4104, Fr-1984 (Atlanta) (10)
$10	GC	1928	A-A	KL-1963, Fr-2400
	SC	1934	A-A	KL-1966, Fr-1701 (8)
		1934-A	B-A	KL-2260, Fr-2309 (No Africa) (9)
	FRN	1928	A-A	KL-1986, Fr-2000 (Boston)
			C-A	KL-1988, (Philadelphia)
			D-A	KL-1989, (Cleveland)
			E-A	KL-1990, (Richmond)

Denomination	Type	Series	Block	Catalog number
			K-A	KL-1996, (Dallas)
		1928-A	B-A	KL-1999, Fr-2001 (New York)
			D-A	KL-2001, (Cleveland)
			E-A	KL-2002, (Richmond)
			G-A	KL-2004, (Chicago)
		1928-B	D-A	KL-2013, Fr-2002 (Cleveland)
			J-A	KL-2019, (Kansas City)
		1928-C	B-A	KL-2022, Fr-2003 (New York) 1934
			B-A	KL-2028,Fr-2005 (New York)
			B-B	(New York)
			D-A	KL-2030, (Cleveland)
			G-A	KL-2033, (Chicago)
		1934-A	A-A	KL-2039, Fr-2006 (Boston)
			B-B	KL-2040, (New York) (6)
			B-C (New York)	
			D-A	KL-2042, (Cleveland)
			G-A	KL-2045, (Chicago)
			G-B (Chicago)	
			L-B	KL-2050, (San Francisco)
		1934-C	G-C	KL-2069, Fr-2008 (Chicago)
		1934-D	B-*	KL-2076*, Fr-2009*(New York)(2)
		1950-A	A-B	KL-2099, Fr-2011 (Boston)
			B-D	KL-2100, (New York)
			G-D	KL-2105, (Chicago)
			H-A	KL-2106, (St. Louis)
		1950-B	G-E	KL-2217, Fr-2012 (Chicago)
		1990	B-A	KL-4001, Fr-2030 (New York)(10)
$20	FRBN	1929	K-A	KL-2272, Fr-1870 (Dallas)
	FRN	1928	F-A	KL-2279, Fr-2050 (Atlanta)
			G-A	KL-2280, (Chicago)
			I-A	KL-2282, (Minneapolis)
			J-A	KL-2283, (Kansas City)
		1934	A-A	KL-2310, Fr-2054 (Boston)
			B-A	KL-2311, (New York)
			E-A	KL-2314, (Richmond)
			G-A	KL-2316, (Chicago)
			J-A	KL-2319, (Kansas City)
		1934-A	A-A	KL-2322, Fr-2055 (Boston)
			B-A	KL-2323, (New York)
			G-A	KL-2328, (Chicago)
			H-A	KL-2329, (St. Louis)
			J-A	KL-2331, (Kansas City)
			L-A	KL-2333, (San Francisco)

Denomination	Type	Series	Block	Catalog number
		1934-B	F-A	KL-2339, Fr-2056 (Atlanta)
			G-B	KL-2340, (Chicago)
		1950-A	B-A	KL-2383, Fr-2060 (New York)
			G-A	KL-2388, (Chicago)
		1985	D-D	KL-3739, Fr-2027(Cleveland)(10)
$50	FRN	1934	B-A	KL-2558, Fr-2102 (New York)
		1934-A	E-A	KL-2572, Fr-2103 (Richmond)
		1974	A-A	KL-2721, Fr-2118 (Boston) (10)
$100	FRN	1934	C-A	KL-2786, Fr-2152 (Philadelphia)
		1996	AD-A	KL-4135, Fr-2175 (Cleveland) (10,11)

SMALL SIZE NATIONAL CURRENCY

Denomination	Series	Charter	Bank name, City, State
$5	1929	I 252	Second National Bank, Pittsburgh, PA
		1741	Crocker First National Bank, San Francisco, CA
		6301	Mellon National Bank, Pittsburgh, PA
		12398	Queensboro Nat'l Bank, New York, NY
		13325	No. Broad Nat'l Bank, Philadelphia, PA
$10	1929-I	121	First National Bank Hartford, CT
		1685	First National Bank, Sharon, PA
		2916	Lake Shore Nat'l Bank, Dunkirk, NY
		7620	Peoples Nat'l Bank, Reynoldsville, PA
		13629	First National Bank, Plainfield, NJ
	1929-II	3623	First National Bank, Dallas, TX
		5065	Ohio National Bank, Columbus, OH

(1) twenty subject uncut sheet plus numerous individual pieces known

(2) "star" or replacement note

(3) most common "Black Eagle" signature combination with inverted back error

(4) cut sheet of four remains intact

(5) contemporary counterfeit known with inverted back

(6) six subject cut half-sheet remains intact

(7) note possesses inverted back and inverted overprint; technically categorized as an inverted second (face) print; only one confirmed

(8) mule and non-mule back designs exist with error

(9) "North Africa" note with yellow Treasury seal; only one confirmed

(10) exhibits faulty alignment appearance on back with portion of adjacent note visible

(11) demonstrates apparent transposed security thread and watermark

EXAMPLES OF THE ERROR

TYPE I

TYPE II

| $1 | SC | 1928-A | Inverted back; star note | R-6 |

Fine: $2500   EF: $3500   CU: $5000

| $1 | SC | 1934 | Inverted back | R-5 |

Fine: $750   EF: $1250   CU: $2000

$1	FRN	1995		Inverted back; Type II		R-5
	Fine: $500		EF: $1000		CU. $1500	

$1	FRN	1999		Inverted back; Type II		R-5
	Fine: $500		EF: $1000		CU: $1500	

$1   FRN   2003-A   Inverted back; Type II   R-6
Fine: $1500   EF: $2500   CU: $4500

$5   FRN   1928-B   Inverted back   R-5
Fine: $500   EF: $1000   CU: $2000

$5   USN   1928-B   Inverted back

Fine: $500   EF: $1000   CU: $2000

$5   SC   1934   Inverted back   R-5

Fine: $500   EF: $1000   CU: $2000

$5   FRBN   1929   Inverted back

Fine: $3500   EF: $5500   CU: $7500

$10   SC   1934   Inverted back   R-5

Fine: $1500   EF: $2500   CU: $3500

$10	FRN	1934	Inverted back	R-5
Fine: $500			**EF: $1000**	**CU: $1500**

$20	FRN	1934	Inverted back	R-5
Fine: $750			**EF: $1500**	**CU: $2000**

$50	FRN	1934-A	Inverted back		R-5
Fine: $2500			EF: $3500	CU: $5000	

$100	FRN	1934-A	Inverted back		R-5
Fine: $3500			EF: $5000	CU: $7500	

Some of God's greatest gifts
are unanswered prayers.
           - Garth Brooks

MISSING PRINTINGS

The missing printing error reaches circulation devoid of an entire impression. Technically, the first, second, or third printing design elements might be absent. However, because the missing overprint error is addressed in a later chapter only notes lacking the first or second printing will be discussed here.

To properly qualify as a missing printing error the note must have completely failed to receive any portion of the intended design at the skipped printing stage. notes which demonstrate even the tiniest portion of the design originate from an alternate etiology and are not classified as missing printings.

There are three distinct causes for a missing printing error. Most commonly, two uncut sheets of currency stock enter the printing press simultaneously with one atop the other. The uppermost sheet accepts the imprint normally while the lower sheet-because it is protected by the top layer-passes through blank. Less frequently, an entire stack of sheets is advanced to subsequent printing and/or cutting operations after skipping a printing stage. Alternate causes of the error are the press operator shutting down the presses in the middle of a run or the printing plates contacting the currency paper and retracting

prematurely. In the later scenarios, the lead portion of the currency sheet will receive impressions from the plate while the tail segment will remain unprinted.

Notes missing the first or back printing are commonly referred to as "blank backs." Notes missing the second or face printing typically enter the overprinting presses normally. This produces a visually spectacular effect with the serial numbers and seals resting in sharp contrast on the white currency paper. All missing printing errors are scarce to rare.

Fractional notes. Aside from pieces intentionally produced as specimens, trials, essays, or proofs there are no known examples of fractional currency without the basic face or back design. Twice a decade a purported "blank back" fractional denomination note surfaces. Thus far, all have represented alterations consisting of carefully split notes.

Large size notes. Two examples of a missing face printing on large size paper money exist. The earliest is a series 1863 $10 which is lacking all of the face design except for the two green "10" counters and the horizontal green bar, both with an engine turned design. As the American Bank Note Company printed the early series, it might have originated from their archives. The other note encompasses an enigmatic specimen of the $500 denomination from the series of 1882 gold certificates. The note lacks the basic face printing, serial numbers, and seal. It displays the word "GOLD" surcharge and the horizontal underlay for the serials, both executed in yellow ink on the front and a normally printed back. Inexplicably, both items show moderate "circulation", which defies explanation. Whether these examples actually represent errors of accidental manufacture or unfinished essays or trial pieces remains subject to debate and further research.

Small size notes. Until the recent past, the missing printing error was extremely rare. There are a miniscule number of blank backs on silver certificates; none on United States notes, gold certificates, national currency, or Federal Reserve bank notes. Fortunately, the large number of missing printing errors on Federal Reserve notes provide collectors with opportunities.

The missing first printing error appears on all seven denominations from $1 through $100. The missing second print remains unknown on the $2 value, but occurs on the other six denominations. The missing first printing or blank back mistake-while scarce in itself-is probably ten times more plentiful than the missing face printing.

A $2 1953-B United States note, missing the first printing, has been authenticated and encapsulated. Careful study of the note, through the holder, certainly points to the genuineness of the piece. It represents the only blank back on any red seal which has withstood scrutiny.

Insights and Incidents. In the Spring of 1995, shortly after the release of the first edition of this book, a group of twenty or so $10 FRN missing the second printing surfaced in the Detroit (MI) area. My father-a fulltime numismatist with four decades of paper money experience-handled many of them. Even that recently, disposing of a dozen or more examples was somewhat of a task. Today, I would relish the opportunity!

Two comments concerning the missing face print: [1] the error remains difficult to locates in dealers' inventories, with many available specimens lightly circulated or drastically overpriced and [2] with the stratospheric levels achieved by other spectacular and dramatic misprints, this eye-popping blunder still seems underpriced. The astute collector might attempt to assemble an eleven piece set from $1 through $100 (minus the deuce) with examples of designs before and after the revamping of small size paper money which began with the series 1996 $100 FRN.

The most exciting discovery in missing face prints appeared in the May, 1998 sale by Currency Auctions of America (CAA). It showcased a $10 star or replacement note minus the second print. Prior to the auction consignment, not even rumors existed about the (thus far) unique error.

A phenomenal trophy was among the Ray Burns collection auctioned by CAA: a genuine blank face-totally blank, not simply missing the second print. In this particular case, the $50 FRN demonstrated a normal first (back) impression, absence of the second print, and application of the third (over) print on the back! A tantalizing assortment of mistakes to create an incredible sequence and outcome. There are presently three known examples from the same half-sheet. One resided in the incomparable Whitney collection, a small portion of which was on exhibit at the 2002 convention of the American Numismatic Association in New York City. The exhibit cleverly utilized a mirror to allow viewers to inspect both sides of the note simultaneously. The incomprehensible display-actually a museum unto itself-won First Place for U.S. Paper Money and also the People's Choice Award.

Over the years, several deceptive pieces-allegedly blank faces-have traded hands. These originated from an East Coast dealer who had six or so in 1981. My opinion was that the pieces represented alterations via mechanical abrasion. This was later confirmed by Bureau of Engraving and Printing personnel who verified surface disturbance with a scanning electron microscope and iron pigment particles (from the removed black ink) via spectroscopy. Unfortunate for the collector who purchased the "error" and submitted it for authentication. The prudent collector considering the purchase of a purported blank face should restrict the search to individual dealers with extensive experience in authenticating error notes and possessing an intimate

working knowledge of paper money production and those willing to provide a refund should the piece later be determined to be an alteration.

The rarity of a missing first printing or blank back error on a star or replacement note cannot be overrated. During the past twenty-seven years, I've seen only eight Most of those involved series 1995 $1 and $10 along with series 1996 $50 and $100. Although expensive, they are tremendously more elusive than the highly touted and higher priced double denominations.

Low-quality alterations of missing printing errors literally flood the internet auction sites, The unscrupulous internet dealers, who hide behind fictitious names use erasers, solvents, and brushes to remove design elements. They start such auctions below face value and offer no return privilege. Only a novice should be caught by their trickery. On the other hand, alterations of exceptional workmanship appear within mainstream sources. While I'm uncertain as to the exact techniques employed to remove the printings, some solvent must be involved. Many of these notes have no smell to them whatsoever. A new piece carries a distinct odor from the paper and inks. The alterations have no discernable odor, as the neutralizer which eliminates or stabilizes the chemicals applied also eliminates the natural odor. Some of these have slipped past personnel at the third party grading services and been encapsulated as genuine. The graders' strength, as a rule, lies in grading paper money, not in authenticating errors.

| $1 | FRN | 19xx | Missing 2nd (face) printing | R-8 |

Fine: $350   **EF: $750**   **CU: $1450**

| $1 | FRN | 1995 | Missing 1st (back) printing; star | R-7 |

Fine: $2500   **EF: $6500**   **CU: $9500**

$1   FRN   1988   Missing 1st (back) printing   R-6
        Fine: $150   **EF: $350**   **CU: $650**

$2   FRN   1976   Missing 1st (back) printing   R-7
        Fine: $2500   **EF: $7500**   **CU: $12,500**

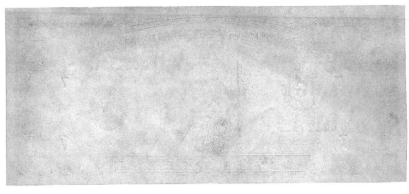

$5   FRN   1977   Missing 1st (back) printing   R-6
        Fine: $150   **EF: $350**   **CU: $650**

$5   FRN   19xx   Missing 2nd (face) printing   R-8

Fine: **$350**   EF: **$750**   CU: **$1450**

$5   FRN   1977   Missing 1st (back) printing; star   R-7

Fine: **$4500**   EF: **$7500**   CU: **$11,500**

$5   FRN   1985   Missing 2ⁿᵈ (face) printing   R-8

Fine: $---   EF: $---   CU: $2500

$10   FRN   19xx   Missing 2nd (face) printing   R-8
       Fine: $350   EF: $750   CU: $1450

$10   FRN   1988-A   Missing 1st (back) printing   R-6
       Fine: $150   EF: $350   CU: $650

$20   FRN   19xx   Missing 2nd (face) printing   R-8
       Fine: $350   EF: $750   CU: $1450

$20	FRN	1977	Missing 1st (back) printing	R-6

Fine: $150   **EF: $350**   **CU: $650**

$20	FRN	1996	Missing 1st (back) printing	R-6

Fine: $250   **EF: $500**   **CU: $850**

$50	FRN	19xx	Missing 2nd (face) printing	R-8

Fine: $1000   **EF: $2000**   **CU: $3500**

$50   FRN   1981-A   Missing 1st (back) printing   R-6
Fine: $500   **EF: $1000**   **CU: $2000**

$50   FRN   1996   Missing 1st (back) printing; star   R-7
Fine: $2500   **EF: $4500**   **CU: $7500**

$100	FRN	19xx	Missing 2nd (face) printing; pre-1996 design	R-8
	Fine: $1000		EF: $2000	CU: $3500

$100	FRN	19xx	Missing 2nd (face) printing; post-1996 design	R-8
	Fine: $1000		EF: $2000	CU: $3500

100	FRN	1996	Missing 1st (back) printing	R-7
	Fine: $500		EF: $1500	CU: $2500

Losing an illusion
makes you wiser than finding a truth.
- Ludwig Borne

MULTIPLE ERRORS

Despite common opinion to the contrary, the occurrence of one error affecting a particular note rarely coincides with the occurrence of a separate error on the same note. A multiple error note shows two or more distinct and unrelated types of mistakes on the same piece of paper money. The errors must arise independent of each other during or between the printing and cutting operations. A combination of even the most common errors on the same note is a prized discovery. The value of the multiple error is not the simple sum of the premium that each error commands. Rather, the value largely remains a matter of agreement between the seller and buyer. The price reflects both the relative scarcity of each mistake and the overall eye appeal of the note.

The scarcity of a single note with multiple errors cannot be overstated. To recognize just how infrequently two distinct errors appear on the same note, the reader is reminded that the chance (or odds) of the joint occurrence equals the frequency of appearance of one error multiplied by the frequency of appearance of the second. With that in mind, one can appreciate the low statistical probability of such an event.

One must consider the production sequence at the Bureau of Engraving and Printing before classifying a note as a multiple error. For example, a large size double denomination with an inverted "back" remains a single error; as it is the transposition of the sheet which begat the double denomination in plate positions A and D. Likewise, on modern FRNs which demonstrate both an inverted overprint and contain a segment of the next note; these Type II inverts result from a trimming or cutting of the top of the sheet prior to the application of the overprint. Such notes are often encountered mislabeled as "double errors" and carrying outrageous prices tags from unknowing or unscrupulous sellers.

Fractional notes. The single most important example of a double error on fractional currency involves inverted corner surcharges on the back coupled with an interior gutter fold visible on the face. Undoubtedly, very few examples of the multiple error exist.

Large size notes. Two examples of multiple errors on large size paper money are known to the author. One is a $1 series of 1917 United States note with an obstructed print through the portrait of George Washington and a fairly reasonable solvent smear on the back. The other is a $1 series of 1923 silver certificate showing minor ink smears and an interior fold on the face. However, there are numerous unconfirmed reports of multiple errors on other pieces of large size paper money.

Small size notes. Aside from a handful of notes bearing an ink smear-gutter fold combination-which seemingly should be the most common multiple error as it is composed of the two most common individual errors-and perhaps a slightly lesser number with an ink smear-faulty alignment or offset printing-gutter fold pairing, the legitimate multiple errors on small size paper money exist in extremely limited quantities. All multiple errors worthy of mention appear on Federal Reserve notes.

Insights and Incidents. Multiple errors are generally under-appreciated in the current market. This phenomenon is likely due to their typically less than spectacular appearance. Too many collectors—especially among those who have entered the error note arena with the past five to ten years—opt for eye appeal above rarity. While everyone drools over visually thrilling mistakes, lesser numbers admire the statistical scarcity of multiple mistakes upon the same piece of paper money. Perhaps it takes a true specialist to fully recognize the excitement that even an ink smear-gutter fold combination should merit. Hopefully, interest in multiple errors will increase but, not too dramatically as there is an insufficient supply.

After a careful analysis it seems that approximately one out of every 125 error notes will classify as a bona fide multiple error.

$1	FRN	1977-A	Multiple error; double 2nd (face) print with ink smears

Fine: $500 EF: **$750** CU: **$1500**

$1	FRN	2003	Multiple error; interior (gutter) fold with sheet misalignment

Fine: $3500 EF: **$10,000** CU: **$15,000**

$5	FRN	1969-A	Multiple error; interior (gutter) folds with ink smear

Fine: $100 EF: **$250**

$10	FRN	1977	Multiple error; double 2nd (face) print with ink smears

Fine: $500   EF: $1500   CU: $2500

$20	FRN	1977	Multiple error; interior (gutter) fold with faulty alignment

Fine: $100   EF: $ 250   CU: $500

If you're going to be thinking anyways, you might as well think big.

- Donald Trump

MULTIPLE PRINTINGS

The multiple printing error bears the normal impression of the first, second, and third printing operations plus a complete or partial extra impression of one of the printings. The error can result from several causes. The most common origin involves a stack of imprinted sheets being re-fed through the press for a printing it has already received. This produces a sheet of notes with two complete images that are separated, as the sheet does not contact the printing plates in the identical location each time. The greater the disparity in the alignment of the subsequent printing, relative to the original impression, the more dramatic and more valuable the error. If the extra impression involves the first or second printing operation, the note usually shows two different plate check numbers on the affected side. When the error appears on the face of the note, it is sometimes referred to as a "four eye" error because the portrait is doubled.

Multiple printings can also occur when a currency sheet enters the press and the press operator stops the machinery. The sheet subsequently returns to the beginning of the press and receives the complete impression of the design on the second pass

through. In this instance, the head portion of the sheet will demonstrate a multiple printing, whereas the tail segment will possess a single impression only. The loose cylinder error is often mistaken for a legitimate multiple printing. With the loose cylinder error, the printing plate "rocks" or "bounces" when contacting the currency paper. This causes a multiple impression with secondary image(s) lighter and ghostlike. Obviously, all images will bear the same plate check number on a given note. When a loose cylinder is responsible, literally hundreds of notes can be affected during one run.

Fractional notes. Salmon P. Chase recommended the use of fractional denominations in paper money and appealed to the United States Congress for approval of the project. Chase recognized the need for government intervention to alleviate the dwindling supply of circulating coinage during the war between the States. Although the proposal was accepted and successfully remedied the problem for several years, the fractional currency series offers only a paltry number of errors. Whether many more mistakes were manufactured and either lost or redeemed (as only a fraction of the original production remains outstanding) or whether the amount known accurately reflects the proportion manufactured will never be known with certainty. Irregardless, at this time there are no documented double printed fractional currency notes.

Large size notes. As with fractional currency, the author is unaware of any multiple printings on large size paper money. The closest that a collector might find is a national currency note with the facsimile signatures of the bank officials stamped more than once. However, because the signatures typically were applied at the individual banking institutions and not within government facilities, such pieces are not generally regarded to be multiple printings.

Small size notes. Herein lie the only examples of the multiple printing error. Small size notes with doubled impressions are extremely rare. They rank among the scarcest of all currency mistakes. The author has observed complete double printed back designs on the $1 and $5 silver certificates (SC) and Federal Reserve notes (FRN), as well as on the $10 through $100 FRN. Complete double second or face printings have been recorded on the $1 SC, $1 through $100 FRN, plus a circulated $2 United States note series of 1928-G. Although scattered examples exist among the early FRN, most come from the series of 1977 and later.

The series of 1950-D $5 FRN from Richmond gave birth to a most unusual multiple printing: four distinct impressions from four different back plates. Inspection of two notes from the same sheet yielded identical results confirming authenticity. From top to bottom, the back plate numbers are: 2429 (lightest impression), 2556, 2481 (strongest impression), and 25xx buried into the design scroll.

In regards to multiple printings of the serial numbers and seals, those on SC and series of 1950 FRN are typically incomplete and greatly shifted horizontally. They remain extremely rare. The few known on later FRN generally appear with the second impression situated above or below the initial printing.

Unarguably, the most visually spectacular of all multiple printings involves the series of 1976 $2 FRN with complete doubling of the overprint. These dramatic examples demonstrate wide separation between the impressions, which are situated one above the other. A limited quantity of nine pieces surfaced in 1986 at the Long Beach (CA) show. A slightly smaller number entered numismatic channels through other sources. The known quantity now rests around two dozen. Since the second edition, researcher Lee Gong has expanded the author's data base. The table appears within this chapter.

Insights and Incidents. The past several years have witnessed an unprecedented number of multiple printings for sale. Not simply the result of the dispersal of a few significant collections but, because of a trickle of individual pieces and small groups of two to six notes. The preponderance demonstrate double impressions of the entire second print, often from two different face plates. Most exhibit minor to moderate separation; a handful of stellar examples show gaps of 4-6 mm between the images.

Another fascinating variant of the multiple printing error is the application of a secondary first (back) printing inverted relative to the primary printing. Harry Jones aptly applied the term "fourth printing" to this mistake. Although four printings exceeds the BEP's intention, his nomenclature cannot be improved.

In the mid-1990s a run of nearly 150 pieces of the series of 1988-A $10 FRN from the A-B block on the Boston district escaped the Bureau bearing multiple impressions of the back design. These notes some rather dramatic-resulted from a loose impression cylinder which created doubled, tripled, or quadrupled images upon contact with the currency paper. To the uninitiated, the mistake appeared to be a multiple printing... and countless examples were advertised and priced as such. The telltale difference among this group is that the secondary, tertiary, and quaternary images are fainter and hazier than the intended printing. Addition-

ally, the back plate check number is the same. Although genuine multiple printings can occur from repeat contact with the identical face or back plate, such occurrences remain less common. Lastly, unless convincing evidence to the contrary exists (for example, different plate check numbers) each image should be of essentially equal darkness.

A final caveat: with the widespread availability of color laser printers and ever-advancing computer technology, the probability of encountering notes altered outside of the BEP increases daily. Thus far, I have examined countless poor and several rather deceptive fabrications. The diagnostic hallmark of a genuine multiple printing is the presence of raised portions of the paper correlating to the intaglio engraving in the printing plates used to impart the back and face designs.

The simplest way to summarize the diagnostic hallmark is:

If the extraneous image lacks embossing, it likely lacks authenticity

As always, the cautious collector acquires notes only from sources expert at differentiating causes and establishing authenticity of error notes. Regrettably, the mere existence of an alleged multiple printing error inside of a third party grading service holder does not, in and of itself, assure the authenticity of the mistake.

SERIAL NUMBER CENSUS OF
$2 1976 DOUBLE THIRD PRINTINGS

D 173 079 22 A (1)	D 228 226 40 A (1)
D 173 079 18 A (2)	D 228 226 36 A (2)
D 173 079 23 A (1)	D 228 226 41 A (1), (3)
D 173 079 19 A (2)	D 228 226 37A (2)
D 173 079 24 A (1)	D 228 226 41 A (1), (3)
D 173 079 20 A (2)	D 228 226 38 A (2), (4)
D 228 225 17 A (1)	D 228 226 42 A (1)
D 228 225 13 A (2)	D 228 226 38 A (2)
D 228 225 18 A (1)	D 228 226 44 A (1)
D 228 225 14 A (2)	D 228 226 40 A (2)
D 228 225 19 A (1)	D 228 226 45 A (1)
D 228 225 15 A (2)	D 228 226 41 A (2)
D 228 225 20 A (1)	D 228 226 46 A (1)
D 228 225 16 A (2)	D 228 226 42 A (2)
D 228 225 21 A (1)	D 228 226 48 A (1)
D 228 225 17 A (2)	D 228 226 44 A (2)
D 228 226 34 A (1)	D 228 226 56 A (1)
D 228 226 30 A (2)	D 228 226 52 A (2)
D 228 226 35 A (1)	D 228 226 60 A (1)
D 228 226 31 A (2)	D 228 226 56 A (2)
D 228 226 36 A (1)	D 228 226 62 A (1)
D 228 226 32 A (2)	D 228 226 58 A (2)
D 228 226 38 A (1)	D 228 226 63 A (1)
D 228 226 34 A (2)	D 228 226 59 A (2)
D 228 226 39 A (1)	D 228 226 64 A (1)
D 228 226 35 A (2)	D 228 226 60 A (2)

(1) Upper serial number
(2) Lower serial number
(3) Two notes with identical upper serial number
(4) Only example known with variance of three, rather than
     four, digits between upper and lower serial numbers

$1 FRN 1977   Double 2nd (face) printing; major R-7
   Fine: $1000   **EF: $2000**   **CU: $3500**

$1 FRN 1963-A   Double 1st (back) printing; partial R-6
   Fine: $250   **EF: $500**   **CU: $1000**

$2 FRN 1976   Double 2nd (face) printing; minor R-8
   Fine: $1000   **EF: $2000**   **CU: $3500**

$2	FRN	1976	Double 3rd (over) printing	R-9
	Fine: $5000		EF: $15,000	CU: $20,000

$5	FRN	1977	Double 2nd (face) printing; major	R-7
	Fine: $500		EF: $1000	CU: $2500

$5	FRN	1950-D	Double 1st (back) printing; minor	R-7
	Fine: $250		EF: $500	CU: $1000

$10   FRN   1950-A   Double 1st (back) printing; minor   R-7
　　　Fine: $500　　　**EF: $750**　　　**CU: $1500**

$20   FRN   1974   Double 3rd (over) printing   R-8
　　　Fine: $5000　　　**EF: $10,000**　　　**CU: $15,000**

$20
FRN
2004
Double printing; series
R-8
Fine: $250
EF: $500
CU: $1000

$50	FRN	1977	Double 2nd (face) printing; moderate	R-7

Fine: $500   **EF: $1000**   **CU: $2500**

$100	FRN	1977	Double 2nd (face) printing; moderate	R-7

Fine: $500   **EF: $1500**   **CU: $2500**

$100	FRN	1950	Double 1st (back) printing; moderate	R-7

Fine: $500   **EF: $1500**   **CU: $2500**

No matter where you go or what you do,
you live your entire life within the confines of your head.
- Terry Josephson

OBSTRUCTED PRINTINGS

Whenever stray material comes between the currency paper and the printing plate during a printing operation, an obstructed printing error occurs. Typically, a scrap of paper lies atop the unfinished sheet of currency stock as it passes through the press. However, other miscellaneous foreign items (such as tissue paper, cellophane, fiber threads, adhesive bandage backings, masking tape, cloth, cardboard, etc.) may be responsible for a blank area on the bill. The design void on the completed note corresponds to the dimensions of the obstructing material.

In the typical scenario, the scrap falls from the currency paper during the subsequent printing, cutting, and packaging stages. If the resulting white space on the note is not detected, the piece enters circulation, while the foreign scrap remains within the Bureau of Engraving and Printing (BEP). On rare occasions, the scrap adheres to the note throughout subsequent printing stages. With the errant material in place, no error may be apparent; however, upon removal the void becomes obvious. By possessing both portions, one is able to recreate and explain the occurrence. The obstructed print error retaining the foreign material ranks among the rarest and most valuable paper money mistakes.

Fractional notes. Even though almost $369 million worth of these odd denomination and miniature size pieces of paper money were printed between 1862 and 1876 (of which about one-tenth of one percent remain unredeemed), the author recalls only three examples of an obstructed print on fractional currency. In terms of sheer size, none is especially exciting. Apparently, the combination of stricter control over debris within the Treasury Department and the lithographic or surface printing method (as opposed to high speed intaglio printing) accounts for the paucity of examples.

Large size notes. Excess clumps of fibers from the pulp utilized to create rolled out currency sheets are responsible for most of the obstructed print errors on horse blanket bills. The thick strands of fibers leave a peculiar, irregularly shaped blank area on the note after separating from it. Unless unusually large, such bills possess a dual problem. They are not dramatic enough for the error collector and too imperfect for the collector of type notes. The obstructed print error caused by redundant fibers appears on virtually every type and denomination of currency manufactured during the production of large size paper money, including a $1000 Federal Reserve note (FRN) series of 1914. However, numerous examples of the obstructed print mistake caused by paper scrap are also known. The most dramatic involves the right end of the face printing on a series of 1917 $1 United States note.

Small size notes. During the early period of small or modern note production, using the wet intaglio process, sheets of non-currency paper were inserted between freshly printed currency sheets to prevent wet ink transfers or offsets of one design onto the adjacent sheet. The currency sheets were stacked with paper tabs between each pile of one hundred sheets. Not infrequently, the tabs slipped into the presses during subsequent printing operations. These rectangular tabs or strips were responsible for the vast majority of the obstructed printing errors that occurred while the wet intaglio process was employed at the BEP. As such, on a percentage basis, obstructed prints appear more commonly on the earlier issues of small size paper money; especially the FRN. However, obstructed printing errors are known on every class of small size paper money, including gold certificates, national currency, and Federal Reserve bank notes. Most obstructed print errors tend to be small and involve only a fraction of the note. Large obstruc-

tions remain rare.

The rarity of a note reaching circulation with the obstructing fragment still adhering cannot be overstated. Since 1995, there has been a release of a modest amount of notes with masking tape alone or in combination with a paper tab. In general, these foreign objects seem to capture a portion of the overprint on the left end. Although slightly more plentiful than previous, neither their relative rarity nor desirability has diminished.

Insights and Incidents. Several spectacular obstructed printing errors surface every year. Not necessarily new examples but, an admixture of specimens eking out from established collections and freshly produced ones escaping the watchful eyes of BEP inspectors.

Even more staggering than the dramatic obstructed prints filtering into the marketplace are the obstruction errors which possess the retained fragment. Historically, these have been exceedingly rare...fully on par with double denominations. However, in recent years the BEP has graciously, but undoubtedly unintentionally-provided a steady trickle of magnificent obstructed printings with the intervening material; yet no new double denominations have been produced in nearly one-quarter century.

An especially interesting variety of the retained fragment is the adhesion of masking tape to the currency sheet before printing; some examples also have a section of light brown to manila color thin cardboard affixed with the tape. One or two dramatic examples of this new type (as opposed to the more traditional obstructions from Kraft paper or scraps of currency stock) appear every six months or so. The collector enamored with this variety of obstructed printings might consider acquiring an attractive piece in the near future, as the BEP likely will implement changes to reduce the release of these pieces.

Unquestionably, the most important obstructed print with retained fragment known surfaced in the summer of 2000. It consists of the complete overprint of a star note on a 3 x 5 index card. The card was so deeply embossed that the host note also demonstrated a blind impression of the third printing, further attesting to the authenticity. Harry Jones and I jointly handled the unique specimen. When it later sold at auction in 2005, the imprinted sscard had been separated from the blindly impressed note.

A modern myth is the existence of a lamination error on paper money. Although a note can be purposely split, the production processes at Crane and Company-which supplies currency stock to the BEP negates the possibility of paper separation. I mention that here as one occasionally encounters obstructed print errors mislabeled as originating from a lamination in the currency stock. This seems especially common when the overprint rests atop a void in the face design. Admittedly, I have never employed a micrometer or scanning electron microscope to evaluate alleged variations in the thickness of a purported lamination error. Nor have I felt the need as a more logical explanation exists. Nearly three decades of involvement in the field of paper money errors have taught me that anything can happen inside the BEP. However, thus far, I have not seen a lamination error on paper money. Caveat emptor.

EXAMPLES OF THE ERROR

MINOR

MODERATE

MAJOR

| $1 | SC | 1928 | Obstructed printing; major | R-5 |

Fine: $350   **EF: $750**   **CU: $1250**

| $1 | SC | 1935-A | Obstructed printing; minor | R-3 |

Fine: $50   **EF: $150**   **CU: $250**

$1
FRN
1995
Obstructed
printing;
with retained
fragment
R-9
Fine: $---
EF: $4500
CU: $7500

$1	FRN	1995	Obstructed printing; minor; star	R-4
	Fine: $150		EF: $250	CU: $500

$1	FRN	2003	Obstructed printing; with retained fragment	R-9
	Fine: $---		EF: $5000	CU: $8500

$2	USN	1953-C	Obstructed printing; minor	
	Fine: $100		EF: $250	CU: $450

$5	FRN	1950-A	Obstructed printing; moderate	R-3

Fine: $100   **EF: $200**   **CU: $350**

$5	FRN	1985	Obstructed printing; moderate	R-3

Fine: $100   **EF: $200**   **CU: $350**

$5
FRN
1985
Obstructed printing; with retained
fragment
R-9

Fine: $---   EF: $4500   CU: $7500

$5	FRN	1985	Obstructed printing; with retained fragment	R-9

Fine: $---   EF: $5000   CU: $8500

$10	SC	1934-C	Obstructed printing; minor	R-3

Fine: $100   EF: $250   CU: $450

$10	FRN	1981-A	Obstructed printing; major	R-5

Fine: $150   EF: $450   CU: $750

$20	FRN	1981	Obstructed printing; with retained fragment	R-9

Fine: $--- EF: $7000 CU: $12,500

$10	FRN	1985	Obstructed printing; with retained fragment	R-9

Fine: $--- EF: $3500 CU: $6500

| $20 | FRN | 1996 | Obstructed printing; with retained fragment | R-9 |

Fine: $---   EF: **$4500**   CU: **$7500**

| $50 | FRN | 1981 | Obstructed printing; with retained fragment | R-9 |

Fine: $---   EF: **$5000**   CU: **$8500**

$100   FRN   1990   Obstructed printing; major   R-5

Fine: $200   **EF: $500**   **CU: $850**

$100   FRN   1996   Obstructed printing; major   R-5

Fine: $250   **EF: $500**   **CU: $850**

*Never stop exploring. If you're
not constantly pushing yourself,
you're leading a numb existence.*

- Dean Karnazes

OFFSET PRINTINGS

Offset printings are impressive currency errors. They look like one side of the note "bled through" to the other. However, an inspection will demonstrate that the offset printing is on the surface and is a mirror image of the note's opposite side. That is, the offset or wet ink transfer places a retrograde image on the wrong side of the bill. Within the printing industry, including the Bureau of Engraving and Printing (BEP), offsets carry the designation of blanket impressions.

A brief review of the printing process will permit the reader to better understand how the error occurs. Under normal operating conditions, a sheet of currency paper passes between the inked printing plate and the impression cylinder. The impression cylinder forces the paper into the intaglio recesses in the printing plate. When the paper fails to enter the press, the plate contacts the impression cylinder. As the next and subsequent sheets of currency paper enter the press, they receive not only the intended printing on the correct side but, on the opposite side a transfer or offset printing as well. This transfer or offset originates from the ink on the impression cylinder. The transferred image becomes lighter with each sheet and disappears entirely after ten to twelve sheets. The rich, bold offset impressions from the first couple of sheets bring the highest prices.

Partial or incomplete offset printings arise in much the same fashion as the complete offsets described above. However, as the name indicates, partial offsets involve merely a portion of the design. An incomplete offset develops when the impression cylinder becomes exposed to part of the inked printing plate through a fold, tear, or defect in a sheet of currency stock. Partial offsets come in an array of sizes and configurations. Their values lie considerably lower than those of complete wet ink transfers.

Although offset printings presently arise in the above manner, such was not always the case. Prior to the introduction of the dry intaglio method of printing at the BEP, notes were produced via the wet intaglio process. The notes were printed on dampened paper, to facilitate the impregnation of the ink into the paper. Consequently, the ink remained moist for a period of time. Sheets of impervious paper were inserted between the freshly printed pages of paper money. When the interleaves were not inserted or improperly aligned, the wet ink transferred directly to another printed sheet. These early offsets are typically much darker than those produced today.

Offsets-complete or partial-of the first printing onto the face, the second printing onto the back, or the third printing onto the back may occur. The so-called back-to-face, sometimes abbreviated B2F, and face-to-back, sometimes abbreviated F2B, offsets are probable to happen in statistically similar numbers. However, because the face of the note is inspected more times than the back, fewer of the back-to-face offsets reach circulation. By far, the offset of the overprint onto the back remains the scarcest.

Fractional notes. Fourteen offset errors on fractional denomination notes have been examined. Nine specimens exhibited an offset of the back printing on the face. Each note was circulated, to one extent or another. One fascinating piece represented a complete ink transfer. Two showed approximately one-half of the design; the remainder displayed only a small portion. Five fractional currency notes exhibited partial offsets of the face printing on the back. None are especially dark.

Large size notes. Numerous examples of partial or incomplete wet ink transfers are known on large size paper money. Predictably, the affected notes favor the later series. The largest offset impression documented covered about 40% of the face on a $1 series of 1923 silver certificate. Another sizeable example exists on a series of 1918 $1 Federal Reserve bank note. Most offsets on large size paper money involve simply a small area along the top, bottom, side margin, or corner. Although none of the contributors to this book recall a complete offset on a large size note, the consensus is that such an error probably exists. Until one is found, the only complete offset that a collector might hope to acquire is a wet ink transfer of the overprint elements onto the back, occasionally encountered on the series of 1923 $1 silver certificates with the Speelman-White signature combination.

Small size notes. Offset printings on small size paper money rank among the most popular of errors. In fact, many neophyte collectors acquire an offset before any other misprint. This is apparently due to the obviousness of this mistake (so blatant that even non-collectors can readily appreciate it) and the affordable price. Wet ink transfers seem relatively common, especially on Federal Reserve notes (FRN). However, especially dark offsets, from the first or second impressions, remain elusive. Complete and partial offsets of the back-to-face, face-to- back, and third printing on back are known on all denominations, on the FRN, from $1 to $100, including the $2. A triangular shaped offset of the face-to-back is known on a series of 1934-A $500. Silver certificates also possess their fair share of offset printing errors; both complete and partial. Partial offsets also exist on gold certificates, national currency, Federal Reserve bank notes, and United States notes.

Fewer complete offsets appear on the re-designed or "big head" currency, introduced with series 1996 $100s and continuing to undergo revision through series 2006 $5s, than on previous FRN. The reason for the diminished number of offsets entering circulation remains unknown as BEP personnel will not divulge the exact changes in electronic or human inspection.

The most intriguing, valuable, and initially perplexing offsets involve two different denominations. These are bona fide double denomination notes yet, sell for a fraction of their more traditional counterparts. Two specimens exist. Both show the back design of one denomination transferred across the face of a different valued note. The potential for a double denomination offset occurs when an inked plate contacts an impression cylinder shortly before the printing plates are changed to another denomination. The first report arrived in 1977. It involved the back of a $20 FRN on the face of a series of 1976 $2 FRN. The second note includes the back of a $1 FRN across the face of a series of 1981 $5 FRN. It was declared genuine by authorities at the BEP.

Insights and Incidents. For years, offsets were, more often than not, the first error purchased by beginning collectors. The enormous eye-appeal coupled with a modest cost enticed many people. The offset served as a springboard to collecting misprints. Somewhere in the mid-1990s, the pendulum swung and the quality of entry level purchases by new collectors escalated. They began to demand more sophisticated mistakes (such as inverted overprints, printed folds, and missing printings) for the initial acquisition. Consequently, there was a temporary surplus of unsold offset printing errors sitting in dealers' inventories. In the late-1990s, due to the popularity of internet sales and on-line auctions, the pendulum swung back and the demand for offsets increased to a level never before achieved. One factor which remained-and continues to remain-constant is the overwhelming favor for early, bold first and second impression transfers. The purchaser needs to understand the experience of the seller in quantifying the darkness of any offset offered. Entirely too often, collectors have been duped into paying unnecessarily high prices for medium or average darkness offsets because the seller has described them as "the darkest ever seen", "extremely sharp, "very bold" or similar hyperbole. Until a seller has seen hundreds, if not thousands, of offset printing errors the potential purchaser should temper any adjectives with skepticism.

Another cause for overwhelming concern is the pseudo-offsets readily generated by image reversal software and a desktop printer. Most personal computers come equipped with software which can reverse an image. By scanning a note, especially the back, reversing the image, sending the image to the printer, and printing it on the face of another note the trouble maker has created the appearance of an offset. Such practice occurs more frequently than the average collector might assume. At almost every major numismatic show, I am offered at least one such "error". Magnification is sometimes beneficial to expose a dot matrix pattern or an image of lesser sharpness than typical. Such shenanigans offer another instance of caveat emptor. Even computer-generated "offsets" occasionally end up in a third-party grading service's holder, underscoring the need to purchase errors only from specialists who will forever guarantee the authenticity of the mistake if you're personally incapable or uncomfortable rendering a definitive opinion prior to buying an "error" from a non-specialist, especially on line.

One of the most important offsets known sold in the Lyn F. Knight auction of the author's collection in 1998. Albeit somewhat light, the piece demonstrated a mirror image of the back of a $1 FRN across the face of a series of 1981 $5 FRN from the Richmond district. A photocopy of the letter of authentication from the BEP accompanied the lot. The amount of circulation (and weakness of the image transfer) enabled the buyer to acquire a legitimate rarity at a reasonable price.

EXAMPLES OF THE ERROR

MINOR

MODERATE

MAJOR

$1   SC   1935-E   Offset; overprinting   R-7
        Fine: $450   EF: $750   CU: $1250

$1   FRN   1963-B   Offset; partial   R-1
        Fine: $15   EF: $25   CU: $50

$1   FRN   1969   Offset; partial   R-1
        Fine: $25   EF: $55   CU: $75

$1   FRN   1969-B   Offset; front to back, complete   R-2
Fine: $75   **EF: $125**   **CU: $200**

$1   FRN   1974   Offset; back to front, complete   R-3
Fine: $75   **EF: $150**   **CU: $250**

$1   FRN   1981-A   Offset; back to front, matte variety R-3
Fine: $75   **EF: $150**   **CU: $350**

$1	FRN	1995	Offset; overprinting, 3rd on back	R-7

Fine: $150   **EF: $350**   **CU: $750**

$2	FRN	1976	Offset; back to front, complete	R-4

Fine: $500   **EF: $1000**   **CU: $1500**

$2	FRN	1976	Offset; roller transfer

Fine: $100   **EF: $200**   **CU: $350**

| $2 | FRN | 1976 | Offset; partial | R-2 |

Fine: $100   **EF: $250**   **CU: $500**

| $2 | FRN | 1976 | Offset; back to front, complete | R-3 |

Fine: $500   **EF: $1000**   **CU: $1500**

| $5 | NBN | 1929 | Offset; overprint |

Fine: $1500   **EF: $2500**   **CU: $3500**

$5	FRN	1974	Offset; front to back, complete	R-2

Fine: $75   EF: **$125**   CU: **$200**

$5	FRN	1981	Offset; back to front, complete	R-3

Fine: $75   EF: **$150**   CU: **$250**

$5	FRN	1981	Offset; overprinting	R-7

Fine: $100   EF: **$250**   CU: **$500**

$10   FRN   1969   Offset; partial   R-1

Fine: $25   EF: $55   CU: $75

$10   FRN   1974   Offset; partial   R-2

Fine: $25   EF: $50   CU: $125

$10   FRN   1981   Offset; overprinting   R-7

Fine: $100   EF: $250   CU: $500

$10   FRN   1985   Offset; back to front, complete   R-3

Fine: $75   **EF: $150**   **CU: $250**

$20   FRN   1977   Offset; front to back, complete   R-2

Fine: $75   **EF: $125**   **CU: $200**

$20   FRN   1981   Offset; back to front, complete   R-3

Fine: $75   **EF: $150**   **CU: $250**

$20	FRN	1981	Offset; partial		R-1
	Fine: $25		EF: $30	CU: $35	

$20	FRN	1996	Offset; back to front, complete		R-3
	Fine: $100		EF: $200	CU: $350	

$20	FRN	1996	Offset; partial		R-1
	Fine: $25		EF: $35	CU: $50	

| $20 | FRN | 1996 | Offset; front to back, complete | R-2 |
| | **Fine: $75** | | **EF: $150** | **CU: $250** |

| $50 | FRN | 1977 | Offset; front to back, complete | R-2 |
| | **Fine: $100** | | **EF: $250** | **CU: $500** |

| $50 | FRN | 1977 | Offset; back to front, complete | R-3 |
| | **Fine: $100** | | **EF: $350** | **CU: $750** |

$100   FRN   1977   Offset; back to front, complete   R-3
        Fine: $250   **EF: $500**   **CU: $750**

$100   FRN   1993   Offset; front to back, complete   R-2
        Fine: $200   **EF: $400**   **CU: $650**

$100   FRN   1996   Offset; back to front, complete   R-3
        Fine: $250   **EF: $500**   **CU: $750**

U. S. BUREAU OF ENGRAVING AND PRINTING. Examining Newly Made Money.

PART THREE

OVERPRINT ERRORS

INVERTED OVERPRINTS

MISALIGNED OVERPRINTS

MISMATCHED SERIAL NUMBERS, CHARTER NUMBERS, AND BLOCK LETTERS

MISSING OVERPRINTS

OVERPRINTS ON BACK

STUCK DIGITS, STUCK BLOCK LETTERS, AND INVERTED BLOCK CHARACTERS

Think like a man of action,
act like a man of thought.
- Henri Louis Bergson

INVERTED OVERPRINTS

Inverted overprints demonstrate the seals and serial numbers upside down relative to the face design. These dramatic errors result from uncut half sheets of currency being inserted into the overprinting presses 180 degrees from the correct orientation. After accepting properly aligned first and second printings, the ends of the uncut half sheets are inadvertently transposed prior to entering the currency overprinting and processing equipment (COPE) for the third or overprinting operation.

On the earlier issues (series of 1935 through 1963-A) of small size notes, the facsimile signatures of the Treasurer of the United States and Secretary of the Treasury and the series designation were applied during the overprinting stage. Thus, they also assumed an inverted position when the error occurred. Since the series of 1963-B Federal Reserve notes (FRN), engravers have reproduced the signatures directly into the intaglio plate used for the second or face printing.

The inverted overprint generated nationwide interest in the field of paper money errors in 1976-78 after unprecedented numbers escaped the Bureau of Engraving and Printing (BEP). Upon release through the Federal Reserve system, the media were inundated with reports of the mistake. A new wave of collecting interest ensued.

Beginning with the series of 1981, the BEP began to trim the selvedge paper from the top of the sheet prior to the third printing; a step previously accomplished after all printings were finished. In the application of an appropriately positioned overprint, the serial numbers and seals fall directly into their designated location. However, when the sheet becomes inverted, the overprint appears to shift towards the bottom of the note. When the upside down half sheets enter subsequent cutting stages-for separation into individual notes-the resulting product contains either a segment of the adjacent note or the upper margin from the sheet at the top. This appearance typifies every inverted overprint beginning with the series of 1981. Robert Azpiazu coined the term "Type II" invert to describe this variety.

Fractional notes. Bronze or gold colored surcharges or overprints - primarily consisting of a large, outlined numeral corresponding to the denomination of the note-were employed on the second and third issues of fractional currency. The overprint was applied to the back of the note by the Treasury Department as an additional measure to discourage counterfeiting. Inverted surcharge printings on fractional currency are scarce. The author estimates the total number in existence at less than one hundred pieces. Nonetheless, a previously unreported specimen seems to surface every year or so.

Large size notes. Unlike the inverted back error, the inverted overprint ranks among the rarest misprints on large size currency. The dramatic effect of upside down serial numbers and seals is seldom witnessed. A mere handful of eleven different examples have traded hands publicly in the past sixty years; perhaps a slightly lesser number, changed ownership privately during the same period. A crisp uncirculated example of the series of 1917 $1 United States notes with an inverted overprint commands a price around twenty thousand dollars--and that represents the only variety regularly encountered in high grade.

Small size notes. Once considered a major rarity, particularly on the higher denomination bills, inverted overprints have flooded the marketplace, particularly back in the 1970s, 1980s, and 1990s. Inverted overprints are most plentiful on FRN, with silver certificates (SC) ranking a moderate second. Scattered examples exist of inverts exist on national currency and United States notes. An inverted overprint on a small size

gold certificate has been reported; its existence remains in question. None is rumored on the Federal Reserve bank notes from the series of 1929 which were printed under emergency financial conditions.

Unlike many types of errors that tend to slip into circulation unnoticed, most inverted overprints on modern paper money are preserved by bank tellers in new condition.

Any attempt to list the known inverted third printings on small size notes would be so extensive, yet so incomplete, as to make the task impractical for the author and unbeneficial for the reader.

Insights and Incidents. In February, 1998 a then new world's record was firmly established for a small size United States paper money error. The magnificent note was a series of 1934-A $5 FRN with inverted brown serial numbers and Treasury seal against black "Hawaii" surcharges. The hammer price was twenty-six thousand dollars plus a ten percent buyer's fee. This demolished the standing record for a small size error note (double denomination $5 face/$10 back series of 1934-D FRN sold by Stack's) by nearly ten thousand dollars. When the note re-sold, exactly seven years later, it fell ten thousand dollars short of its high-water mark. It later exceeded its previous auction level

Interest in upside down third printings flourishes among collectors, especially with the myriad possibilities available. Since the publication of the first edition, several significant changes in United States paper money production and design have transpired. One change, the trimming of the top of the uncut sheet prior to the final print, directly affects the appearance of inverted overprints. These Type II inverts contain either a portion of the adjacent note or the upper margin of the uncut sheet at the top. Such notes are not double (or multiple) errors-contrary to the hype espoused by non-specialists. I've engendered more heated debates about this topic than all other aspects of paper money errors combined!

The contemporary collector enjoys a greater spectrum of inverted overprints than ever before. Obviously, fractional currency, large size, and small size SC, FRN, United States notes, and national currency inverts have been around for one-half century. However, the Type II invert-coupled with the ongoing designs changes-makes the permutations nearly endless. No longer should one aspire to merely acquire a denomination set of $1 through $100 FRN but, collect the aforementioned in Type I and Type II plus inverted overprints on the redesigned FRN.

A final commentary: as the designs continue to undergo changes, with distinct varieties appearing every year or so, the collector would do well to purchase an example of any error, at a reasonable price, rather than wait to see how common a given mistake becomes on a given design and denomination.

As this edition approaches publication, a previously unknown inverted overprint of magnificent eye-appeal and incomparable rarity was consigned for auction. The note, a $100 1966 USN star replacement, is likely to establish a new record for the error type.

TABLE OF INVERTED OVERPRINTS

FRACTIONAL CURRENCY

Denomination	Issue	Catalog number
5c	2nd	KL-3226, Fr-1232
		KL-3227, Fr-1233
10c	2nd	KL-3230, Fr-1244
		KL-3231, Fr-1245
		KL-3232, Fr-1246 (1)
		KL-3233, Fr-1247
		KL-3235, Fr-1249
	3rd	KL-3262, Fr-1255 (2)
		KL-3263, Fr-1256 (3)
25c	2nd	KL-3236, Fr-1283
		KL-3237, Fr-1284
		KL-3239, Fr-1286
		KL-3241, Fr-1288
		KL-3242, Fr-1289
		KL-3243, Fr-1290
	3rd	KL-3265, Fr-1291
		KL-3268, Fr-1294
		KL-3270, Fr-1296
		KL-3271, Fr-1297
		KL-3272, Fr-1298
50c	2nd	KL-3245, Fr-1316
		KL-3246, Fr-1317
		KL-3247, Fr-1318
		KL-3250, Fr-1321
		KL-3251, Fr-1322
	3rd	KL-3283, Fr-1331
		KL-3284, Fr-1332
		KL-3285, Fr-1333
		KL-3286, Fr-1334
		KL-3287, Fr-1335
		KL-3288, Fr-1336
		KL-3289, Fr-1337
		KL-3290, Fr-1338
		KL-3291, Fr-1339
		KL-3292, Fr-1340
		KL-3293, Fr-1341
		KL-3294, Fr-1342
		KL-3312, Fr-1360
		KL-3314, Fr-1362

Denomination	Issue	Catalog number
		KL-3315, Fr-1363
		KL-3316, Fr-1364
		KL-3317, Fr-1365
		KL-3318, Fr-1366
		KL-3319, Fr-1367
		KL-3320, Fr-1368
		KL-3321, Fr-1369
		KL-3322, fr-1370
		KL-3323, Fr-1371
		KL-3324, Fr-1372
		KL-3325, Fr-1373

LARGE SIZE NOTES

Denomination	Type	Series	Catalog number
$1	SC	1899	KL-49, Fr-234
		1923	KL-52, Fr-237
	USN	1917	KL-23, Fr-36
			KL-25, Fr-38
	FRBN	1918	KL-66, Fr-713 (New York)
			KL-72, Fr-719 (Cleveland)
			KL-79, Fr-726 (Atlanta)
			KL-96, Fr-743 (San Francisco)
			KL-97, Fr-744 (San Francisco)
$2	SC	1899	KL-139, Fr-258
$5	SC	1899	KL-241, Fr-271
	FRN	1914	KL-279, Fr-851 (New York)
			KL-283, Fr-855 (Philadelphia)

SMALL SIZE NATIONAL CURRENCY

Denomination	Series	Charter	Bank name, City, State
$5	1929-I	2154	First National Bank, Belleville, NY
		6499	Farmers Merchants National Bank, Tyrone, PA
		12352	Liberty Nat'l Bank Trust Company, New York, NY
$10	1929-I	1085	National Bank of, Wrentham, MA
		8390	First National Bank, Guttenberg, NJ

SMALL SIZE "HAWAII" NOTES

Denomination	Type	Series	Block	Catalog number
$1	SC	1935-A	S-C	KL-1609, Fr-2033 (4)
$5	FRN	1934-A	L-A	KL-1961, Fr-2302 (5)
$10	FRN	1934-A	L-A	KL-2258, Fr-2303 (4)
$20	FRN	1934-A	L-A	KL-2524, Fr-2305 (4)

(1) uncut blocks of nine and four known, plus uncut pair, and several singles

(2) inverted overprint varieties, on this number include: inverted face surcharge, inverted back surcharge, and inverted face and back surcharges

(3) inverted face and back surcharges

(4) inverted black "HAWAII" surcharge on back; four or five known

(5) inverted brown serial numbers and Treasury seal; two known

EXAMPLES OF THE ERROR

TYPE I

TYPE II

$1	SC	1934	Inverted overprint	R-5
	Fine: $3500		EF: $5500	CU: $7500

$1	SC	1935-D	Inverted overprint; signatures and series	
	Fine: $2000		EF: $3500	CU: $5000

$1	SC	1935-E	Inverted overprint	R-5
	Fine: $750		EF: $1500	CU: $2000

| $1 | FRN | 1974 | Inverted overprint | R5 |
| Fine: $200 | | EF: $350 | | CU: $500 |

| $1 | FRN | 1985 | Inverted overprint; Type II | R-5 |
| Fine: $250 | | EF: $450 | | CU: $850 |

| $1 | FRN | 1988-A | Inverted overprint; web | R-6 |
| Fine: $2500 | | EF: $3000 | | CU: $4500 |

$2   USN   1953   Inverted overprint

Fine: $15,000   **EF: $20,000**   CU: $25,000

$2   FRN   1976   Inverted overprint   R-6

Fine: $1000   **EF: $2000**   CU: $3000

$5   NBN   1929   Inverted overprint

Fine: $35,000   **EF: $50,000**   CU: $---

$5	FRN	1934-A	Inverted overprint; Hawaii
Fine: $---		**EF: $---**	**CU: $25,000**

$5	SC	1934-C	Inverted overprint	R-5
Fine: $2500		**EF: $6500**	**CU: $9500**	

$5	FRN	1950-A	Inverted overprint; star note	R-6
Fine: $2500		**EF: $4500**	**CU: $7500**	

| $5 | SC | 1953 | Inverted overprint | R-5 |

Fine: $2500   EF: $6500   CU: $9500

| $5 | FRN | 1974 | Inverted overprint | R-5 |

Fine: $250   EF: $450   CU: $850

| $5 | FRN | 1985 | Inverted overprint; Type II | R-5 |

Fine: $250   EF: $450   CU: $850

| $10 | FRN | 1950-A | Inverted overprint; star note | R-6 |
| Fine: $2500 | | EF: $4500 | CU: $7500 | |

| $10 | SC | 1953-A | Inverted overprint | R-5 |
| Fine: $5000 | | EF: $15,000 | CU: $20,000 | |

| $10 | FRN | 1999 | Inverted overprint; Type II | R-5 |
| Fine: $350 | | EF: $850 | CU: $1250 | |

| $20 | FRN | 1934-B | Inverted overprint; green portion only | R-5 |
| | **Fine: $2500** | | **EF: $7500** | **CU: $12,500** |

| $20 | FRN | 1988-A | Inverted overprint; Type II | R-5 |
| | **Fine: $250** | | **EF: $500** | **CU: $850** |

| $50 | FRN | 1977 | Inverted overprint | R-5 |
| | **Fine: $350** | | **EF: $750** | **CU: $1500** |

$50   FRN   1996   Inverted overprint; Type II   R-5

Fine: **$500**   EF: **$1500**   CU: **$2500**

$100   FRN   1977   Inverted overprint   R-5

Fine: **$350**   EF: **$750**   CU: **$1750**

$100   FRN   1996   Inverted overprint; Type II   R-5

Fine: **$500**   EF: **$1500**   CU: **$2500**

*The philosophers have only interpreted the world...
the point however is to change it.*

- Karl Marx

MISALIGNED OVERPRINTS

Misaligned overprint errors are readily recognized by the eccentric placement of the final printing elements. Typically, this involves the serial numbers and seals. The overprint may assume a skewed or shifted orientation.

The apparent shift in the overprint on the completed note usually results from the improper feeding of the currency sheet into the overprinting press. The sheet enters the final printing operation at an angle or with unequal amounts of paper on the right and left sides. The overprint shift may also arise from an existing fold in the currency paper that affects the dimensions of the uncut half sheet and consequently alters the relative position of the notes receiving the final printing. In the former instance, each note on the sheet will bear a nearly identical misalignment; in the later, the degree of the shift will be a function of the note's relation to the fold.

For a misalignment to legitimately qualify as an error, a portion of the overprint must rest atop a portion of the design it was not intended to cover. Despite excellent quality control within the Bureau of Engraving and Printing (BEP), minor variances

in position are within acceptable tolerance limits.

Shifts with the overprint abnormally close to the right end of the note are the most common. Those towards the bottom rank a distant second. Vertical shifts in an upward direction fall close behind. While shifts with the overprint misaligned to the left end are by far the least common.

Fractional notes. Despite the typically high production and inspection standards maintained within the Treasury Department during the issuance of fractional currency-which probably accounts for the relatively miniscule supply of other types of errors-misalignment of the overprint or surcharge elements is a commonly found mistake. In fact, slightly out of position overprints are so common as to pose a dual problem. They appeal to neither the error collector, who seeks a more striking example, nor to the non-error collector who desires a more ideally placed overprint. While the minor shifts are commonplace, truly major misalignments are elusive. Minor misalignments are known for every type of note printed with a surcharge; whether the overprint is the large outlined numeral on the back corresponding with the denomination, the bronze oval surrounding the portrait on the face, or the designators in the corners on the back. Moderate to major misalignments are known on the more common fractional currency designs, in limited quantities.

Large size notes. The author remains aware of a few examples of a major shift of the overprint on a piece of large size paper money. One is a series of 1899 $1 silver certificate. Although only in very fine condition, the note also bears a courtesy autograph of a Treasury official. The other variety-of which three specimens from the same sheet of four are known-is the series of 1923 $1 United States note with an enormous upward shift in the red Treasury seal and large numeral "1".Since the publication of the second edition, a wonderful example of a series 1899 $2 silver certificate shift has come to light. There are unconfirmed reports of two major shift errors on national currency from the series of 1902. This phenomenon seems perplexing as missing overprint and inverted overprint errors, which should have proven easier for the inspectors to catch, are seen on occasion. Even a moderately mis-positioned overprint on large size currency would be a prized discovery.

Small size notes. Minor shifts in the overprinting occur so often on small size paper money that many continue to pass through circulation, even among those alert enough to identify the error. However, truly major misalignments-in terms of distance or angle-remain important enough to capture the attention of the numismatic press. Moderate to major shifts in the overprinting elements are known on all six classes of small size notes including gold certificates and Federal Reserve bank notes, which are frequently exempt from other types of mistakes. All six examples from the same sheet of series 1929 $5, from The Chase National Bank of the City of New York, bearing the most dramatic shift on national notes are known. These rank among the most desirable misaligned overprints on small size notes.

Insights and Incidents. Misaligned overprints-or "shifts" in the common vernacular-remain popular, with the wildest mal-positions most actively pursued. Truly fantastic shifts with enormous displacements or bearing portions of overprints from two or more separate notes prove to be exceedingly rare and command prices commensurate with their scarcity. A candidate for the most spectacular example of a misaligned overprint surfaced in October of 2000. The note, a series of 1974 $1 FRN from the Cleveland district, contains a horizontal shift so enormous that the right side of the note bears the black district seal and serial number (intended for the left end); the left side carries a green Treasury seal and serial number from the left end of the adjacent note on the uncut half sheet. I enjoyed the privilege of purchasing the error from the discoverer, through an intermediary, and selling it to another specialist.

Although, in general, errors on two dollar notes are more difficult to locate than on other denominations such is definitely not the case with minor misalignments of the overprint. Minor shifts (particularly in a downward direction with the serial numbers barely contacting the words "Washington, D.C.") are extremely common on series of 1976 FRN. Although the uniformed and the unscrupulous attempt to overstate the rarity, especially on internet auction sites, such minor shifts prove unexciting to the knowledgeable collector.

Star or replacement note errors capture special attention and garner an extra premium. Nonetheless, overall star note errors remain under priced in relation to their relative rarity. Misaligned overprints are no exception. A major mal-position of the overprint on a star note should be aggressively pursued by all collectors needing a representative example. On star notes, stupendous shifts are nearly as elusive as inverted overprints...of which a mere handful exists.

EXAMPLES OF THE ERROR

MINOR

MODERATE

MAJOR

$1   SC   1935-E   Misaligned overprint; one color   R-3
      Fine: $500   **EF: $1500**   **CU: $2500**

$1   FRN   1977-A   Misaligned overprint; one color   R-3
      Fine: $50   **EF: $150**   **CU: $350**

$1   FRN   1981   Misaligned print; major   R-4
      Fine: $750   **EF: $1500**   **CU: $3500**

$1	FRN	1981	Misaligned overprint; major	R-4
	Fine: $250		EF: $500	CU: $1500

$1	FRN	1981-A	Misaligned overprint; moderate	R-2
	Fine: $50		EF: $100	CU: $250

$1	1985	FRN	Misaligned print; minor	R-1
	Fine: $10		EF: $25	CU: $50

$1   FRN   1995   Misaligned overprint; one color   R-3
Fine: $50   EF: $100   CU: $200

$2   FRN   1976   Misaligned overprint; moderate   R-3
Fine: $50   EF: $100   CU: $250

$2   FRN   1995   Misaligned overprint; one color   R-4
Fine: $250   EF: $500   CU: $1000

$1	FRN	1981	Misaligned overprint; major	R-5

Fine: $500   EF: $1000   CU: $2500

$5	FRN	1950-A	Misaligned overprint; moderate	R-2

Fine: $50   EF: $100   CU: $250

$5	FRN	1969	Misaligned overprint; moderate	R-2

Fine: $50   EF: $100   CU: $250

$10	FRN	1934-A	Misaligned overprint; one color	
Fine: $750			EF: $1500	CU: $2500

$10	FRN	1950-D	Misaligned overprint; major	R-4
Fine: $250			EF: $500	CU: $750

$10	FRN	2001	Misaligned overprint; one color	R-3
Fine: $500			EF: $1000	CU: $1500

$10   FRN   2001   Misaligned overprint; major   R-4

Fine: $250   EF: $750   CU: $1500

$20   FRN   1974   Misaligned overprint; moderate   R-2

Fine: $100   EF: $250   CU: $350

$20   FRN   1999   Misaligned overprint; major   R-4

Fine: $250   EF: $500   CU: $1000

| $20 | 2001 | FRN | Misaligned print; minor | R-1 |
| | Fine: $25 | | EF: $50 | CU: $100 |

| $50 | FRN | 1969 | Misaligned overprint; moderate | R-2 |
| | Fine: $150 | | EF: $250 | CU: $750 |

| $100 | FRN | 1996 | Misaligned overprint; moderate | R-2 |
| | Fine: $150 | | EF: $200 | CU: $350 |

Satisfaction lies in the effort, not in the attainment.
- Mahatma Gandhi

MISMATCHED SERIAL NUMBERS, CHARTER NUMBERS, and BLOCK LETTERS

Mismatched serial numbers have plagued United States currency since its introduction. However, it took the abundant production and extensive publicity of the U 37xx/ U 47xx mistake on the series of 1957-B $1 silver certificate (SC) to popularize the error.

In those instances where the lower left serial number differs from that in the upper right position, either manual or mechanical factors are at fault. Most numbering irregularities stem from a press operator failing to set the same sequence of numbers on the two different numbering wheels prior to initiating a printing run. Under this circumstance, the mismatch is typically evident among the digit(s) in the beginning of the serial number, while those digits towards the right end are identical. Examples of this manual mistake in the press set-up are the U 37xx/ U 47xx, G 55xx/G 54xx, and the A 97250xx/ A 86139xx errors. Mismatched serial numbers will happen also when one numbering machine sticks at a particular serial number,

while the other continues to advance normally. Under this scenario, the error is evident among the digit(s) at the ends of the serial numbers, with those at the beginning being identical. Examples of this mechanical mistake in one of the numbering wheels are the xx49 I/xx50 I, xx815 C/xx700 C, and xx595 A/xx601 A errors.

Aside from mismatched serial numbers, other numbering or lettering irregularities infrequently occur. The Albert A. Grinnell collection contained a series of 1902 $10 note of the First National Bank of Bay Shore, New York with charter number 10026 on the left side and charter number 10029, the correct one, on the right. Two examples of mismatched charter numbers are known on the series of 1902 $5 from the National Bank of Savannah, Georgia. These show charter number 3046 on the left side and charter number 3406, the correct one, on the right. The error further is documented on a small size note from the First National Bank in

Tigerton, Wisconsin. It exhibits charter number 14150, the correct one, on the left side and charter number 12150 on the right. More careful examination of national currency presently residing in collections might add to the current list.

Prefix and suffix letters-the characters immediately preceding and following the serial number-are also subject to mismatch. Two different "blocks" (a block being the combination of the prefix and suffix letters on a given note) result from human error during the press set-up. The mistake appears on nearly twenty separate series. The most startling being the uncut sheets of series of 1981 $1 Federal Reserve notes (FRN) sold directly to the public by the Bureau of Engraving and Printing (BEP).

Fractional notes. Serial numbers were not used on fractional currency.

Large size notes. Despite the millions of large size notes printed in numerous design types over a span of almost three-quarters of a century, the two serial numbers rarely lost synchronization; a mere dozen or so examples have been reported.

The earliest mismatches known appear on the series of 1862 $1 United States notes. Since the Albert A. Grinnell sales of the 1940s, a solo specimen was recorded. However, subsequent to the publication of the first edition of this book, a second piece has surfaced in the estate of a prominent stamp collector in Texas; it remains ensconced.

Later large size issues are lightly sprinkled with numbering irregularities: the series of 1899 $1 "Black Eagle" and $5 "Chief Onepapa" SC and the series of 1917 $1 United States note. In the past ten years, both a series of 1923 $1 SC and a series of 1902 national currency bearing mismatched serial numbers have appeared at public auction. No doubt the subtle nature of the error, incomplete records, and attrition have removed additional serial number discrepancies from the domain of the modern researcher and collector. Mismatched serial numbers on large size notes rightfully carry a price comparable to the double denomination error. They reside among the most expensive paper money misprints.

Small size notes. The government first released small size paper money into circulation on January 10, 1929-after pondering the concept for more than fifteen years-as a measure to reduce printing and paper expenses. Shortly after the debut, the first numbering error occurred. Approximately one hundred fifty distinct mismatches exist on at least seven different denominations, including the series of 1934 $1000 FRN. The mistake affects every class of small size paper issued since the series of 1928, with the possible exception of the Federal Reserve bank notes.

FRN capture the lion's share of the mismatched serial numbers. SC follow closely behind. The $1 and $5 denominations account for most of the discoveries. The majority of mismatches involve a single digit discrepancy. However, both a series of 1928 $10 FRN on the Chicago district and a series of 1977-A $1 FRN on the

Boston district have the first five numerals mismatched.

As a general rule, the production of a particular mismatch amounts to just a few pieces; although a couple of notable exceptions exist. Literally thousands of the U 37xx/U 47xx mistakes escaped on the series of 1957-B $1 SC. Nearly fifty years after their discovery, one consecutively numbered pack of one hundred bills remains extant. A somewhat similar event transpired in the summer of 1963 when almost ten thousand $1 SC from the series of 1957-bearing serial numbers beginning G 55xx on the left and G 54xx on the right-were released from storage at Fort Benning, Georgia. Even though a large number of G 55xx/ G 54xx errors circulated, many reached the numismatic marketplace unimpaired. On FRN, the most abundant mismatched serial number produced, with quantities in the thousands, is the series of 1969 $1 starting with F 68xx on the left and F 67xx on the right. In 1992 a tremendous amount of mismatched serial numbers of the series of 1976 $2 FRN was discovered. These xx523 A/ xx623 A errors, from the New York district, provided a bonanza for collectors who previously had been unable to secure an example of the error on the two dollar denomination. A somewhat smaller number surfaced with mismatched prefix letters. Unless a particular mismatch is printed and released in large numbers, so that astute bank tellers and cash handlers can procure uncirculated specimens, the error typically enters commerce before being noticed.

The following lists of mismatched serial numbers, charter numbers, and block letters are undoubtedly incomplete. This compilation simply includes the varieties documented at the time of publication. Unquestionably other mismatches exist. Their absence does not imply any greater rarity than those recorded.

Insights and Incidents. In the early 1980s, I owned and advertised four of the then seven known mismatched serial numbers on large size paper money. Two originated from the estate of Amon G. Carter, Jr. One, a gem crisp uncirculated $1 series of 1862 (Fr-16) appeared at a Kagin's auction held during the Memphis Paper Money Show. The other, a low grade series of 1862 $2 United States note (Fr-41) arrived via private treaty with a prominent dealer. The other two (a series of 1917 $1 United States note (Fr-39) and a three digit mismatch on a series of 1923 $1 SC (Fr-237)) left an advanced New England collection. Nearly thirty years later, all four pieces continue to reside in a prominent Manhattan collection.

Although the above recollection serves as a reminder of foregone days, it pales in comparison to the incident related by Harry Jones. He reported that a United States serviceman stationed in Germany discovered two packs of the mismatched $2 series of 1976 FRN. Being unfamiliar with the numismatic fraternity, the serviceman's wife flew the notes from Germany to the United States to accept payment and complete the transaction! Undoubtedly, if a miniscule number of specimens had surfaced, the price tag might create sticker shock. Instead, ample mismatches exist on the series of 1976 $2 FRN from the New York district to suppress the cost to a modest level.

Newly discovered mismatched serial numbers surface with some regularity; combining new releases with older notes coming to light for the first time. A typical quantity consists of a mere one to four pieces. A thrilling exception is the series of 1988 $1 FRN star or replacement notes with a two digit mismatch created at the Fort Worth facility. A truck stop operator in Arkansas found forty-seven consecutive notes in a pack. I was fortunate enough to handle nearly all of those released into the numismatic marketplace.

The series of 1934 $1000 FRN mismatch carries a most unusual history. John Rowe, at the roundtable discussion sponsored by Lyn F. Knight during the auction of the Frank Levitan collection in December of 1998, provided the details. The mismatch, originally owned by William Philpott, served as the catalyst to terminate "Mr. Phil's" relationship with a Federal Reserve bank branch. He lost a valuable source; wherein the pioneer paper money dealer could acquire crisp uncirculated large size notes at face value as needs dictated. The note was subsequently sold as a unique $1000 mismatch; which it remains until this day. The significance of the piece was later forgotten. It later re-sold as a generic high denomination note. In the ensuing years, the mismatch was once again discovered. A diligent east coast collector spent more than ten years-and a consider-able sum of money-to acquire it in 2000. Hopefully, the importance of this unique error will not again become lost.

A seasoned and observant veteran of paper money collecting "cherry picked" a rare mismatched block error on a $10 series of 1929 national currency from an internet auction site at a price commensurate with a common type note. His success should enthuse all collectors. Knowledge remains king.

Since the release of the 2nd edition, I purchased a veritable hoard of $1 mismatched serial numbers. *Three consecutive packs* of $1 series 1981-A, from the Atlanta district, were sold by the original discoverer who had salted them away for more than two decades. This previously rare mistake was promoted on cable television to buyers outside of mainstream collecting; despite the three hundred additional notes, the number available to collectors hasn't changed. However, the Relative Rarity Index has been changed to reflect this discovery.

In September of 1983, a customer deposited ten series 1977 $50 notes, with the A-* / K-* mismatched prefix into the Middleburg Office of the Tri-County National Bank in Pennsylvania. The Executive Committee, at the bank, authorized the sale of seven pieces at face value to employees on a first come, first served basis. Apparently all were purchased, as I later bought one from a teller who provided a copy of the memorandum. Interestingly, no mention is made as to the disposal of the other three pieces.

TABLE of MISMATCHED SERIAL NUMBERS

LARGE SIZE NOTES

Denomination	Type	Series	Left serial	Right serial	Catalog number
$1	USN	1862	40863	40857	KL-3, Fr-16
			40857	40853	
		1869	Z8203467*	Z8203471*	KL-5, Fr-18
		1917	H65400001A	H65410001A	KL-24, Fr-37
			R22514789A	R22514791A	KL-27, Fr-39 (1)
			R22514791A	R22514793A	
	SC	1899	R78755400	R78755398	KL-43, Fr-228
			D11506050A	D11507050A	KL-48, Fr-233
			D38477001A	D38476001A	
		1923	B68073098D	B68073102D	KL-52, Fr-237
$2	USN	1862	90890	96890	KL-100, Fr-41
$5	SC	1899	M82762358	M82762354	KL-248, Fr-278
					Charter number, Bank name, City, State
$5	NC	1902	11200	10200	Ch-8411 First Nat'l Bank, Sabina, OH (2)

SMALL SIZE NOTES

Denomination	Type	Series	Left serial	Right serial	Catalog number
$1	SC	1934	A84xxx561A	A83xxx651A	KL-1451, Fr-1606
			Dxxxxxx28A	Dxxxxxx38A	
		1935-A	I524xxxxxB	I525xxxxxB	KL-1453, Fr-1608
			Txxxxxx12C	Txxxxxx32C	
			Xxxxxxx38B	Xxxxxxx28C	
			Yxxxxxx76B	Yxxxxxx66B	
		1935-B	Hxxxxxx06D	Hxxxxxx16D	KL-1454, Fr-1609 (3)
		1935-C	Pxxxx4009D	Pxxxx3993D	KL-1455, Fr-1612
			T009xxxxxD	T000xxxxxD	
		1935-D	B0736xxxxF	B0735xxxxF	KL-1456, Fr-1613(W)
			Bxxxxxx76G	Bxxxxxx86G	KL-1456-A, Fr-1613 (N)
			K6975xxxxG	K6976xxxxG	
			Wxxxxxx68F	Wxxxxxx58F	(4)
			Xxxxxxx76F	Xxxxxxx86F	

Denomination Type	Series	Left serial	Right serial	Catalog number
	1935-E	*35xxxxxxD	*34xxxxxxD	KL-1457-*, | Fr-1614-*
		A19xxxxxxH	A29xxxxxxH	KL-1457, Fr-1614
		Axxxxxx95H	Axxxxxx79H	
		Dxxxxxx49I	Dxxxxxx50I	
		F84xxxxxxI	F86xxxxxxI	
		G25xxxxxxH	G14xxxxxxH	
		Nxxxxx205H	Nxxxxx198H	(5)
		Sxxxxx814H	Sxxxxx956H	
		X53xxxxxxG	X54xxxxxxG	
		Y3xxxxx61[]	Y2xxxxx70G	(6)
		Z160xxxxxG	Z161xxxxxG	
	1935-F	*xxxxxx42F	*xxxxx32F	KL-1458-*, Fr-1615-*
	1935-G	*xxxxxx30G	*xxxxx28G	KL-1459-*, Fr-1616-*
		Dxxxxxx51J	Dxxxxxx41J	KL-1459, Fr-1616
	1957	G55xxxxxxA	G54xxxxxxA	KL-1462, Fr-1619
		U261xxxxxA	U260xxxxxA	
	1957-A	D4662xxxxA	D4663xxxxA	KL-1463, Fr-1620
	1957-B	*xxxxxx67A	*xxxxxx47A	KL-1464-*, Fr-1621-*
		*xxxxxxx0B	*xxxxxxx8B	
		*xxxxxxx1B	*xxxxxxx0B	
		Sxxxxxx55A	Sxxxxxx48A	KL-1464, Fr-1621
		U37xxxxxxA	U47xxxxxxA	
FRN	1963	Axxxxx961*	Axxxxx849*	KL-1465-*, Fr-1900-* (Boston)
		Bxxxxxx65A	Bxxxxxx75A	KL-1466, (New York)
		Bxxxxxxx2A	Bxxxxxxx1A	
		Bxxxxx821A	Bxxxxx921A	
		Hxxxxxx15A	Hxxxxxx24A	KL-1472, (St. Louis)
		H87xxxxxxA	H89xxxxxxA	
		Lxxxxx814B	Lxxxxx924B	KL-1476, (San Francisco)
	1969	F68xxxxxxA	F67xxxxxxA	KL-1506, Fr-1903 (Atlanta)
	1969-A	D42xxxxxxB	D32xxxxxxB	KL-1516, Fr-1904 (Cleveland)
	1969-B	Bxxxxxxx7C	Bxxxxxxx5C	KL-1526, Fr-1905 (New York)

Denomination Type	Series	Left serial	Right serial	Catalog number
	1969-D	B760xxxxxC	B761xxxxxC	KL-1562, Fr-1907 (New York)
		B44xxxxxxD	B43xxxxxxD	
		Cxxxx7900B	Cxxxx8000B	KL-1563, (Philadelphia)
		G0xxxxxxxC	G9xxxxxxxC	KL-1567, (Chicago)
	1974	B760xxxxxC	B761xxxxxC	KL-1574, Fr-1908 (New York)
		D2409xxxxA	D2400xxxxA	KL-1576, (Cleveland)
		D8888xxxxA	D8889xxxxA	
		Exxxx4665D	Exxxx6665D	KL-1577, (Richmond)
		E3700xxxxD	E3702xxxxD	
		E75xxxxxxD	E74xxxxxxD	
		F800xxxxxC	F801xxxxxC	KL-1578, (Atlanta)
		G539xxxxxB	G530xxxxxB	KL-1579, (Chicago)
	1977	B666xxxxxF	B667xxxxxF	KL-1586, Fr-1909 (New York)
		E0020xxxxE	E0022xxxxE	KL-1589, (Richmond)
	1977-A	A97250xxxB	A86139xxxB	KL-1597, Fr-1910 (Boston)
	1981	Exxxxx095B	Exxxxx195B	KL-3504, Fr-1911 (Richmond)
		F522xxxxxE	F511xxxxxE	KL-3505 (Atlanta)
		J47xxxxxxB	J37xxxxxxB	KL-3509 (Kansas City)
	1981-A	F7003xxxxB	F7002xxxxB	KL-3605, Fr-1912 (Atlanta)
		F99xxxxxxD	F98xxxxxxD	K6696xxxxB K6697xxxxB KL-3610, (Dallas)
	1985	E03xxxxxxG	E33xxxxxxG	KL-3704, Fr-1913 (Richmond)
		F31xxxxxxG	F21xxxxxxG	KL-3705, (Atlanta)
		Lxxxx5574A	Lxxxx5474A	KL-3711, (San Francisco)
	1988-A	G11xxxxxx*	G00xxxxxx*	KL-3850-*, Fr-1915-* (Chicago) (7)

Denomination	Type	Series	Left serial	Right serial	Catalog number
			G2590xxxxA	G2599xxxxA	KL-3850, Fr-1915 (Chicago)
		1995	=I73707330N	I06030650N	KL-4092, Fr-1922 (Minneapolis) (8)
		1999	A1xxxxxxxC	A0xxxxxxxC	KL-4174, Fr-1923 (Boston)
			Bxxxxx282J	Bxxxxx442J	KL-4175, (New York)
		2001	Bxxxxx857B	Bxxxxx907B	KL-4187, Fr-1927 (New York)
			Hxxxxxx85A	Hxxxxxx22 A	KL-4292 (St. Louis)
			I985xxxxxA	I984xxxxxA	KL-4293 (Minneapolis)
		2003-A	Bxxxxx288B	Bxxxxx388B	KL-, Fr-1930 (New York)
$2	FRN	1976	Bxxxxx523A	Bxxxxx623A	KL-1628, Fr-1935 (New York) (9)
			F7001xxxxB	F7000xxxxB	KL-1632, (Atlanta)

					Charter number, Bank name, City, State
$5	NC	1929-I	C000001A	C001001A	Ch-5089, Milliken National Bank, Decatur, IL

					Catalog number
	USN	1928	Axxxxxx27A	Axxxxxx21A	KL-1639, Fr-1525
		1953	A1009xxxxA	A1000xxxxA	KL-1646, Fr-1532
			Axxxxxx40A	Axxxxxx30A	
	SC	1934-D	Dxxxxx579A	Dxxxxx601A	KL-1655, Fr-1654
		1953	Axxxx7000A	Axxxx6000A	KL-1656, Fr-1655
			A4774xxxxA	A4775xxxxA	
			Axxxxx211A	Axxxxx100A	
	FRN	1950	Gxxxxxx19A	Gxxxxxx29A	KL-1797, Fr-1961 (W), (Chicago)
		1950-A	Bxxxxx801C	Bxxxxx700C	KL-1804, Fr-1962 (New York) (10)
			Cxxxxx835A	Cxxxxx935A	KL-1805 (Philadelphia)
			Exxxxxx98A	Exxxxxx99A	KL-1807 (Richmond)

Denomination	Type	Series	Left serial	Right serial	Catalog number
			Fxxxxx085B	Fxxxxx193B	KL-1808 (Atlanta) (11)
			H4038xxxxA	H4039xxxxA	KL-1810 (St. Louis)
			H84xxxxxxA	H48xxxxxxA	
			Jxxxxxx71A	Jxxxxxx81A	KL-1812 (Kansas City)
			Lxxxx6003B	Lxxxx6000B	KL-1814 (San Francisco)
		1950-B	Ixxxxxx39A	Ixxxxxx46A	KL-1823, Fr-1963 (Minneapolis)
		1950-C	Gxxxx9009D	Gxxxx8979D	KL-1833, Fr-1964 (Chicago)
		1969	Cxxxxxx11A	Cxxxxxx00A	KL-1878, Fr-1969 (Philadelphia)
		1969-A	I2291xxxxA	I2290xxxxA	KL-1896, Fr-1970 (Minneapolis)
		1974	I611xxxxxA	I612xxxxxA	KL-1932, Fr-1973 (Minneapolis)
			J36xxxxxxB	J35xxxxxxB	KL-1933, (Kansas City)(12)
		1977-A	E0409xxxx*	E0408xxxx*	KL-1952-*, Fr-1975-* (Richmond)
			Hxxxx6125A	Hxxxx5292A	KL-1955, Fr-1975 (St. Louis) (13)
			L44xxxxxxA	L45xxxxxxA	KL-1959, (San Francisco)
		1981	B44xxxxxxB	B45xxxxxxB	KL-3513, Fr-1976 (New York)
		1985	Gxxxxx700B	Gxxxxx630B	KL-3718, Fr-1977 (Chicago)
		1988-A	D68398xxxB	D68399xxxB	KL-3859, Fr-1980 (Cleveland)
		1995	E010xxxxxC	E001xxxxxC	KL-4100, Fr-1984 (Richmond)
$10	FRN	1928-B	G44460xxxA	G35208xxxA	KL-2016, Fr-2002 (Chicago)
		1950	J2951xxxxA	J2950xxxxA	KL-2096, Fr-2010 (W) (Kansas City)
		1950-A	Bxxxx6999C	Bxxxx7000C	KL-2100, Fr-2011 (New York)
			Dxxxxxx66A	Dxxxxxx65A	KL-2102, (Cleveland)

Denomination	Type	Series	Left serial	Right serial	Catalog number
			E0111xxxx*	E0110xxxx*	KL-2103-*, (Richmond)
			Fxxxxx355*	Fxxxxx407*	KL-2104-*, (Atlanta) (14)
			Fxxxxxx90B	Fxxxxxx23B	KL-2104,
		1950-B	Cxxxxx591*	Cxxxxx691*	KL-2113-*, Fr-2012-* (Philadelphia)
		1950-D	E110xxxxx*	E111xxxxx*	KL-2139-*, Fr-2014-* (Richmond)
		1963-A	E63xxxxxxA	E64xxxxxxA	KL-2166, Fr-2017 (Richmond)
		1985	Ixxxxxx23A	Ixxxxxx13A	KL-3732, Fr-2027 (Minneapolis)
		1990	H3639xxxxA	H3635xxxxA	KL-4007, Fr-2030 (St. Louis)
					Charter number, Bank name, City, State
$20	NC	1929-I	Bxxx221A	Bxxx187A	Ch-1487, First National Bank of Red Wing, MN
					Catalog number
	GC	1928	Axxxxxx29A	Axxxxxx28A	KL-2261, Fr-2402
	FRN	1934-A	Gxxxxx609*	Gxxxxx585*	KL-2328*, Fr-2055* (Chicago)
		1950-A	Axxxxxx34A	Axxxxxx33A	KL-2382, Fr-2059 (Boston)
		1950-C	Fxxxxxx30B	Fxxxxxx29B	KL-2411, Fr-2062 (Atlanta)
		1977	G4506xxxxB	G4507xxxxB	KL-2517, Fr-2072 (Chicago)
			Lxxxxxx63A	Lxxxxxx27A	KL-2522 (San Francisco)
		1981-A	B10xxxxxxD	B00xxxxxxD	KL-3637, Fr-2075 (New York)
		1993	Jxxxx1957A	Jxxxx1657A	KL-4057, Fr-2079 (Kansas City)

Denomination	Type	Series	Left serial	Right serial	Catalog number
		1996	AL7861xxxxF	AL7862xxxxF	KL-4713, Fr-2083 (San Francisco)
		2004	ED26xxxxxxC	ED27xxxxxxC	KL-, Fr. 2089 (Cleveland)

					Charter number, Bank name, City, State
$100	NC	1929-I	B000064A	B000062A	Ch-2604, Winters Nat'l Bank & Trust Co Dayton, OH

					Catalog number
	FRN	1985	B0599xxxxA	B0589xxxxA	KL-3761, Fr-2171 (New York)
		1996	AB152xxxxxS	AB156xxxxxS	KL-4133, Fr-2175 (New York)
			ABxxxxx658X	ABxxxxx648X	
$1000	FRN	1934	Hxxxxxx67A	Hxxxxxx37A	KL-3004, Fr-2211 (St. Louis)

$1	SC	1957	Mismatched serial; G 55/G 54	R-4

Fine: $150   **EF: $350**   **CU: $650**

$1	SC	1957-B	Mismatched serial; U 37/U 47	R-4

Fine: $150   **EF: $350**   **CU: $650**

$1	FRN	1969	Mismatched serial; F 68/F 67	R-4

Fine: $150   **EF: $350**   **CU: $650**

$1   FRN   1969-B   Mismatched serial; 02 C/00 C   R-5
    Fine: $250   **EF: $450**   **CU: $850**

$1   FRN   1969-D   Mismatched serial; B 44/B 43   R-5
    Fine: $250   **EF: $450**   **CU: $850**

$1   FRN   1981-A   Mismatched serial; F 98/F 99   R-4
    Fine: $250   **EF: $450**   **CU: $950**

$1   FRN   1981-A   Mismatched serial; F 98/F 99
three consecutive packs

$1 FRN 1988-A Mismatched serial; G 11-*/G 00-* R-6

Fine: $1000 EF: $2500 CU: $3500

$1 FRN 2001 Mismatched serial; 682 B/962 B R-5

Fine: $150 EF: $350 CU: $650

$2 FRN 1976 Mismatched serial; 542 A/ 642 A R-4

Fine: $150 EF: $350 CU: $650

$5	NBN	1929	Mismatched serial; 0001 A/ 1001 A	
Fine: $---		**EF: $---**	**CU: $65,000**	

$5	FRN	1950-A	Mismatched serial; 862 C/700 C	R-5
Fine: $500		**EF: $1000**	**CU: $1500**	

$5	FRN	1974	Mismatched serial; J 36/J 35	R-5
Fine: $150		**EF: $350**	**CU: $650**	

$5   FRN   1977-A   Mismatched serial; 6122 A/4288 A R-5
Fine: $500   **EF: $1000**   **CU: $1500**

$5   FRN   1977-A   Mismatched serial; L 44/L 45   R-4
Fine: $150   **EF: $350**   **CU: $650**

$5   FRN   1985   Mismatched serial; 77 B/07 B   R-5
Fine: $250   **EF: $450**   **CU: $850**

$10	FRN	1963-A	Mismatched serial; E 63/E 64	R-5

Fine: $500   **EF: $1000**   **CU: $1500**

$20	FRN	1981-A	Mismatched serial; B 10/B 00	R-5

Fine: $500   **EF: $1000**   **CU: $2000**

$100	NBN	1929	Mismatched serial; 64 A/62 A

Fine: $---   **EF: $45,000**   **CU: $---**

TABLE of MISMATCHED CHARTER NUMBERS

LARGE SIZE NOTES

Denomination	Series	Charter number	Bank name, City, State
$5	1902-DB	Ch-3406	Nat'l Bank, Savannah, GA (1)
	1902-DB	Ch-1205	Mechanics & Metals Nat'l Bank New York, NY (2)
$10	1902-DB	Ch-10029	First Nat'l Bank, Bay Shore, NY (3)

SMALL SIZE NOTES

Denomination	Series	Charter number	Bank name, City, State
$5	1929-II	Ch-11978	First Nat'l Bank Ashland, VA (4)
$10	1929-II	Ch-14150	First Nat'l Bank Tigerton, WI (5)

(1) correct charter number (3406) on right; incorrect number (3046) on left; at least two examples documented

(2) correct charter number (1250) in six positions along border; both overprinted charter numbers (3557) incorrect

(3) correct charter number (10029) on right; incorrect (10026) on left

(4) correct charter on black overprint (11978); incorrect (11878) adjacent to both serial numbers

(5) correct charter number (14150) near left serial number and both black overprints; incorrect (12150) preceding right serial number

$10	BBB	1828	Mismatched charter	
	Fine: $8500		EF: $14,500	CU: --

TABLE OF MISMATCHED BLOCK CHARACTERS

SMALL SIZE NOTES

Denomination	Type	Series	Left block	Right block	Catalog number
$1	SC	1935-E	Y-[]	Y-G	KL-1457, Fr-1614 (1)
		1957	A-A	Q-A	KL-1462, Fr-1619
			M-A	M-A	(2)
	FRN	1969-B	C-C	B-C	KL-1526, Fr-1905 (New York)
		1977-A	B-D	A-D	KL-1597, Fr-1910 (Boston)
		1981	A-H	B-H	KL-3500, Fr-1911 (Boston) (3)
		1988-A	K-G	L-G	KL-3854, Fr-1915 (Dallas)
		1995	A-C	K-G	KL-4094, Fr-1922 (Dallas) (4)
			I-E	-I-E	KL-4092 (Minneapolis)(5)
			=I-N	I-N	
		1999	C-E	C-I	KL-4176, Fr-1923 (Philadelphia)
$2	FRN	1976	H-A	B-A	KL-1628, Fr-1935 (New York)
$5	SC	1953-A	D-A	A-A	KL-1657, Fr-1656
	FRN	1950-B	D-B	E-B	KL-1819, Fr-1963 (Richmond) (6)
		1981	J-A	K-A	KL-3521, Fr-1976 (Kansas City)
		2003-A	FI-A	FH-A	KL- , Fr-1991 (St. Louis)

					Charter number, Bank name, City, State
$10	NC	1929-I	B-A	E-A	Ch-200, First Nat'l Bank, Boston, MA
			B-A	A-A	Ch-9077, Farmers & Merchants Fort Branch, IN

					Catalog number
	FRN	1981	I-*	L-*	KL-3532, Fr-2025 (Minneapolis)
			K-B	L-B	KL-3534 (Dallas)
		1995	E-C	-E-C	KL-4112, Fr-2033 (Richmond)
$20	FRN	1996	AK-A	AK-A	L-12 designator: KL-4713, Fr-2083 (Dallas)
$50	FRN	1977	A-*	K-*	KL-2733-*, Fr-2119-* (Boston)
$100	FRN	1996	AC-A	AG-A	KL-4138, Fr-2175 (Chicago)

(1) solid, rectangular suffix character on left; note also contains mismatched serial numbers

(2) right serial number bears an inverted "W" instead of the correct "M" prefix; error occurs in positions E2 and E4 only

(3) exists only on uncut sheets sold to the public by the BEP; plate position G3

(4) prefix and suffix letters mismatched; correct block is K-G as note bears district seal and numbers for Dallas

(5) some also demonstrate a seven digit mismatch within the serial number

(6) "D" prefix rotated downward

$1	FRN	1995	Mismatched block; -I-N/I-N	R-7
Fine: $1000		**EF: $1500**	**CU: $2000**	

$1	FRN	1999	Mismatched block; C-E/C-I	R-7
Fine: $1500		**EF: $2500**	**CU: $4500**	

$2	FRN	1976	Mismatched block; H-A/B-A	R-6
Fine: $250		**EF: $500**	**CU: $850**	

| $20 | FRN | 1996 | Mismatched block; AK-A/L-12 | R-7 |

Fine: $1500   **EF: $3500**   **CU: $5500**

| $50 | FRN | 1977 | Mismatched block; A-*/K-* | R-8 |

Fine: $2500   **EF: $5500**   **CU: $8500**

Nobody made a greater mistake than he who did nothing because he could only do a little.

- Edmund Burke

MISSING OVERPRINTS

The missing overprint error lacks the application of the third printing elements on the note. Typically, such notes do not demonstrate the serial numbers and seals; although the series designation and facsimile signatures were included in the overprinting process through the series of 1963-A. The missing overprint error possesses only the basic green back and black face printings. It looks very much like "play money."

The error develops from any of four separate causes. The most frequent etiology is the feeding of two uncut half sheets through the overprinting press simultaneously. The uppermost sheet makes contact with the overprinting machinery and accepts the impression. While the bottom sheet is protected during the printing operation and transported to the cutting knives without the elements of the third print. An alternate origin lies in a single half sheet entering the overprinting press properly but, the press fails to engage and impart the serial numbers and seals. Another cause for the error is the accidental advancement of a stack or pallet of currency sheets from the second or face printing presses directly to all ensuing cutting operations. In this instance, a large quantity of missing overprints

will be created. The last explanation for the mistake is a major obstructed print, where either a large fragment of foreign matter or a major fold elsewhere in the sheet covers enough of one or more notes to capture the entire overprinting. If the foreign matter dislodges prior to entering circulation or the sheet unfolds prior to the cutting operation, the note escapes without any indication as to the actual cause. There is no variance in the pricing structure of missing overprints based upon presumed causes for the mistake.

Fractional notes. Overprints were added to the backs of notes during the second and third issues. One was a large, outlined numeral that corresponded to the value. This final printing step offered another measure to combat the rampant counterfeiting of the era. The omission of the value overprint on fractional currency was an apparently rare event. Less than six examples are known to the author, all in circulated condition. The mistake of omitting minor overprints on the corners of the backs was much more frequent.

Large size notes. Extensive research reveals that the missing overprint error on large size paper money is more common than one might suspect. Throughout the sixty-eight years of production, the mistake affected a host of denominations and types. The missing overprint error-like most blunders on large size notes-appears most often on the $1 bills of later series. Whether this reflects the increased manufacture of currency, which allowed more opportunities for accident, or increased sloppiness within the government facilities remains open to conjecture.

Because the note looks essentially complete to the untrained eye and due to the periods of economic hardship during which the pieces were printed, most circulated at least briefly. Caution must be exercised in contemplating the purchase of a missing overprint error in well worn condition. Some notes which have been available suggest possible evidence of tampering to selectively remove the overprint elements.

Small size notes. Although the missing overprint rightfully commands a respectable premium, this type of paper money mistake exists in relatively plentiful numbers. Small size notes missing the third printing are known for every denomination of Federal Reserve note (FRN) from the $1 through $100, including a handful of examples of the $2. Gold certificates, silver certificates (SC), national currency, Federal Reserve Bank notes, and United States notes also fell victim to the error.

The missing overprint typically affects a 16 subject half-sheet. Therefore the quantity released is a usually a multiple of 16, rather than a solo piece or random amount as in some other types of errors. On the early series of FRN and SC, inspectors at the Bureau of Engraving and Printing (BEP) sometimes wrote the correct (yet missing) serial number on the sheet when it was discovered to be devoid of an overprint. Some of these annotated errors accidentally reached circulation; including six consecutive series of 1928-A $1 SC which remain intact.

During the 1930s and 1940s, many missing overprint errors passed freely through multiple transactions before being retrieved from circulation. Economic hardships, fear of holding a perceived counterfeit note, and lack of familiarity with paper money of the realm likely contributed to the unabated spending. However, in today's more error-conscious society, most notes lacking the serial numbers and seals frequently are preserved in uncirculated condition.

Printing changes at the BEP-which began with the redesigned series of 1996 $100 FRN-now include the application of the green Treasury seal separate from the black universal Federal Reserve seal and green serial numbers. Consequently, a missing overprint on the redesigned paper can encompass a note bearing a Treasury seal but, lacking the serial numbers and black seal. As production within the BEP continues to evolve, by necessity, so does our definition of certain error types.

Notes lacking only the green Treasury seal have entered the market unabated since thousands of examples of the series 1996 $20 were released along the Atlantic seaboard. Aside from the twenty dollar denomination, a near equal quantity of $100s have escaped, with small numbers on other denominations.

Insights and Incidents. In 1998, I advertised a small size series of 1928 gold certificate missing the overprint. The note graded extremely fine. It originated from face plate 53 and back plate 71, as is the case with the few others known from the six subject half sheet. It was priced at nine hundred dollars in the *Bank Note Reporter*. Although I clearly recognized the rarity, I markedly underappreciated its market value…as a deluge of potential orders confirmed. Only months later, a crisp uncirculated example sold for $17,600 in a Currency Auctions of America sale. Even the "experts" make mistakes, even while making a profit!

An alarming increase in altered large size notes, purporting to possess a missing overprint error-have appeared for sale at auction, on fixed price lists, and in dealers' inventories. Either the high prices error notes command in the current market have drawn long held pieces out from various collections or modern charlatans are chemically removing BEP-applied overprints to dupe the wave of new collectors. Perhaps an unhealthy dose of skepticism has caused me to silently denounce an occasional genuine error as phony. On the other hand, I'd much prefer to err on the conservative side than purchase a possibly altered piece. I suspect that most collectors share similar sentiments. Unfortunately, too many accept, as gospel truth, opinions advanced by sellers with inadequate

experience in the specialized arena of error notes. The purchaser must remain ever-vigilant, especially when examining a heavily circulated example. Of particular suspicion are large size notes missing the red overprint. Over the years, I've seen many such pieces lacking thered Treasury seal, yet demonstrating an impression or embossing of the same. In speaking with experts in paper restoration, I've learned that the red ink "slips" much more easily than any other color, so most of the pieces advertised as errors represent, in reality, alterations.

The color shift ink, positioned in the lower right corner on the face of the note, technically qualifies as an overprint as it is not part of the basic back or face printings. This anti-counterfeiting device, with numerals equivalent to the denomination, was introduced with the series of 1996 $100 redesigned FRN. Literally hundreds of pieces exist on the $100; a much smaller number appear on the $20. The missing color shift ink error proved so unpopular with collectors that one dealer elected to spend his inventory of thirty-some pieces, at a loss, rather than continue to tie up working capital.

To witness the handiwork of crooks—and the uneducated that they deceive—surf onto any internet auction site where paper money is listed alongside of countless other categories. There you'll find altered notes being offered as genuine missing overprint errors. In particular, the scoundrels tend to remove the black portion of the overprint, as it doesn't lie on top of a printed design.

$1	SC	1928	Missing overprint		R-6
	Fine: $500		EF: $1500	CU: $2500	

$1	FRN	1977	Missing overprint		R-6
	Fine: $100		EF: $200	CU: $450	

$1	FRN	1999	Missing overprint; one color; star	R-5
	Fine: $250		EF: $650	CU: $1000

$2   FRN   1976   Missing overprint   R-7
        Fine: $1500   EF: $4500   CU: $7500

$5   FRN   1985   Missing overprint   R-6
        Fine: $100   EF: $200   CU: $450

$10   FRN   1934-C   Missing overprint; one color   R-4
        Fine: $1000   EF: $2500   CU: $4500

$10	FRN	1977	Missing overprint	R-6

Fine: $100   EF: $200   CU: $450

$20	FRN	1981	Missing overprint	R-6

Fine: $150   EF: $250   CU: $500

$20	FRN	1996	Missing overprint; one color	R-4

Fine: $200   EF: $450   CU: $850

| $20 | FRN | 1996 | Missing overprint | R-6 |
| | | | | |

Fine: $200   EF: $450   CU: $850

| $50 | FRN | 1985 | Missing overprint | R-6 |

Fine: $350   EF: $750   CU: $1250

| $50 | FRN | 1996 | Missing overprint | R-6 |

Fine: $350   EF: $750   CU: $1500

$100   FRN   1969-C   Missing overprint   R-6

Fine: $500   EF: $1500   CU: $2000

$100   FRN   1996   Missing overprint   R-6

Fine: $500   EF: $1500   CU: $2000

If your success is not on your own terms,
if it looks good to the world but does not feel good
in your heart, it is not success at all.

- Anna Quindlen

OVERPRINTS on BACK

Not surprisingly, the overprint on back error demonstrates the third printing elements on the back of the note. The serial numbers, Treasury seal, and, if applicable, the Federal Reserve bank or universal seal and corresponding district numerals appear on the wrong side. The error develops when an uncut half sheet enters the overprinting press with the back-instead of the face-closest to the printing heads. This produces a note with the appearance of a mistake on both sides. The face, which lacks the third printing elements, resembles "play money," with a sharp contrast between the black ink of the second printing and the white currency paper. The back, which carries the third printing elements, seems too crowded as portions of the overprint rest atop and blend into the ornate design.

The overprint on back error and the inverted overprint error captured headlines in numismatic and daily newspapers in 1976 and 1977 when unprecedented numbers were released from the Federal Reserve banks. These dramatic blunders sparked a major interest in error currency.

Fractional notes. Errors in the overprints applied to this class of paper money account for the greatest percentage of mistakes. These surcharge errors take many forms including: missing (especially the characters in the corners on the back), misaligned (common on the bronze oval on the face), and inverted (rarest on the denomination designator on the back). However, aside from essays and specimens, the appearance of an overprint on the wrong side of an issued fractional currency note remains unknown.

Large size notes. Overprint elements on the back of a large size note resulting from a four subject uncut sheet being inserted into the press wrong side up are also unknown. Both wet ink transfers or offsets and printed folds have caused complete or partial overprints to appear on the back but, these represent different types of errors. In the wet ink transfer, the third print exists in a mirror or retrograde image. In the printed fold, a crease is evident in the currency paper. The fold, when opened, separates the portion of the overprint present on the back from that on the face.

Small size notes. Despite the sophisticated electronic sensors of the currency overprinting and processing equipment (COPE)-which intend to eliminate and identify the manufacture of errors during the final printing, cutting, and banding operations-the overprint on back error now escapes in almost sufficient quantity to satisfy collector demand. Prior to the introduction of the COPE, fewer examples of the overprint on back escaped the watchful eyes of seasoned inspectors. The series of 1974 and later Federal Reserve notes (FRN) offer the only readily available pieces.

The error appears with approximately equal frequency on all denominations, proportionate to the number of notes produced, with the exception of the $2 value. Only six to nine examples of the third print on back exist on the series of 1976 $2 FRN; thus far, none are known on the series of 1995, 2003, or 2003-A. The second scarcest denomination is the $50; followed by the $100.

The overprint on back error is scarce on silver certificates. It is unknown on national currency, gold certificates, United States notes, and Federal Reserve bank notes.

Insights and Incidents. Error notes demonstrating the overprint on the incorrect side remain as popular as ever. Collectors can begin to assemble denomination sets of FRN-from $1 to $100, minus the deuce-on both old and redesigned paper money. Such an assortment would make quite a display!

In reference to the $2 FRN, six pieces with the third print on the back were unleashed by a bank in rural Indiana in 1995. I handled the notes; all continue to reside in advanced collections. Like other mistakes (most notably the blank back), certain misprints were essentially unknown on $2 FRN until banks began clearing out stagnant supplies of the bicentennial issue to make room for the unequally unpopular series of 1995.

There was no such bonanza created when banks cleared out existing supplies of the series 1995 to create vault room for the series 2003 and then later the series 2003-A.

Perhaps the most intriguing-and unarguably the rarest-notes bearing the overprint on the back are star or replacement pieces. Exactly two pieces have been verified: a $5 FRN and $20 FRN. The former sold at auction in February, 1998; the later reposed in the most advanced collection of overprint mistakes ever amassed until the assemblage was sold intact.

The inverted overprint on back appears to be a major "sleeper" among United States paper money mistakes. Unless the BEP ferrets out additional examples, existing pieces should prove to be extremely rare. Even if the Bureau accommodates collectors' desires, new examples are most likely to appear on the redesigned FRN. Four of the $20 FRN with an inverted orientation of the third print on the back-all from the same half sheet-surfaced in metropolitan Detroit. Interestingly, each note went to different coin dealers before I acquired them.

In March of 2001, a series of 1988-

A FRN, printed on the web press, containing the overprint on the back surfaced...more than a decade after its accidental manufacture. The note originated from run 8 of the G-P block and carries the 5/8 combination of face and back plates. Within ten days, rumors of a second piece-arising within a 100 mile radius of the location of the discovery note-started. The rumors proved to be unfounded.

However, since that time, a few more examples have been confirmed.

Also discovered since the publication of the second edition has been a handful of series 1977-A $1 FRN printed on experimental Natick test paper. Undoubtedly more remain to be identified by collectors knowledgeable about this poorly publicized experiment.

SERIAL NUMBER CENSUS OF OVERPRINTS ON BACK

FOR $1 1977-A NATICK TEST PAPER

E 78779660 II
E 78879760 H
E 78879666 H
E 78879670 H
E 78979672 H
E 78979675 H
E 79059666 H
E 79059668 H

SERIAL NUMBER CENSUS OF OVERPRINTS ON BACK

FOR $1 1988-A "WEB" PRESS NOTES

A 03573561 F
A 03773561 F
A 04173561 F
A 04373561 F
G 48133051 P
G 48533051 P
G 48733051 P
G 48933051 P

$1	FRN	1977-A	Overprint on back	R-5

Fine: $150   **EF: $250**   **CU: $450**

$1	FRN	1988-A	Overprint on back; web press	R-6

Fine: $1500   **EF: $3500**   **CU: $5000**

$1	FRN	1995	Overprint on back; inverted	R-8

Fine: $1000   **EF: $1500**   **CU: $2750**

$2	FRN	1976	Overprint on back	R-6
	Fine: $2500		EF: $7500	CU: $12,500

$5	FRN	1981	Overprint on back	R-5
	Fine: $150		EF: $300	CU: $500

$5   FRN   1981-A   Overprint on back; star note   R-6
Fine: $2500   EF: $5000   CU: $8500

| $10 | FRN | 1977-A | Overprint on back | R-5 |

Fine: **$150**   EF: **$300**   CU: **$500**

| $10 | FRN | 2001 | Overprint on back; inverted | R-8 |

Fine: **$1000**   EF: **$1500**   CU: **$2750**

$20   FRN   1985   Overprint on back   R-5

Fine: **$150**   EF: **$300**   CU: **$500**

$20	FRN	1996	Overprint on back	R-5
	Fine: $250		EF: $500	CU: $750

$50	FRN	1985	Overprint on back	R-5
	Fine: $250		EF: $500	CU: $1000

$50	FRN	1996	Overprint on back	R-5
	Fine: $250		EF: $750	CU: $1500

$100   FRN   1990   Overprint on back   R-5
        Fine: $500   EF: $1000   CU: $1750

$100   FRN   1996   Overprint on back   R-5
        Fine: $750   EF: $1500   CU: $2500

*The easiest part of life is living. It's living with yourself,
after the way you choose to live it, that's hardest.*

- Marielle Alcantara

STUCK DIGITS STUCK BLOCK LETTERS, and INVERTED BLOCK CHARACTERS

Stuck digit errors are sometimes called partially turned digits, although the two terms actually represent different forms of a similar mistake affecting the serial number. The stuck digit error demonstrates parts of two different digits in the same position. It transcends two sequential numbers, with the bottom portion of the higher number at the top and the lower number at the bottom. The partially turned or rolled digit error evidences only one digit rotated upwards and out of alignment with the margins of the adjacent numerals.

Both the stuck digit and partially turned digit result from a clogging of the numbering wheel on the cylinder that imprints the serial number. If the wheel freezes into place in a particular position, each successive note will appear identical. If, however, the wheel initially locks into place to print a partially turned digit and later advances just slightly a stuck digit might result. These are mechanical malfunctions which arise during a printing run and generally do not

result during the press set-up. Stuck digits are of a rarity comparable to the more popular mismatched serial numbers. As such, they remain under-priced in the marketplace relative to their actual scarcity.

Stuck block letters and their counterparts, partially turned block letters appear identical as the stuck digits and partially turned digits described above. However, these commonly occur due to failure of the press operator to accurately align the prefix and suffix letters prior to initiating a run. Although stuck and partially turned digits occur with some mild regularity, similar errors affecting the alphabetical characters preceding and following the numerals prove extremely difficult to secure.

Inverted block letters develop when a press operator manually inserts the alphabetical character or star upside down prior to initiating a run. Like the stuck digits, partially turned digits, stuck block letters, and partially turned blocks, this error occurs in only one position on the uncut half sheet.

Fractional notes. This class of paper money obviously remains exempt from these errors as the currency was printed without serial numbers.

Large size notes. Examples of the partially turned or rolled digit appear frequently on large size notes, most especially the series of 1923 $1 silver certificates (SC). In fact, even moderate rotations of a single digit or suffix letter are so commonplace as to be non-collectible as errors. The stuck digit, however, provides a formidable challenge. The author documents a sole example of a legitimate stuck digit with portions of two numerals in the same position. There are unconfirmed reports of three or four others.

Stuck and inverted block letters continue to be unreported on large size paper money.

Small size notes. Locating a specimen of the partially turned digit error should present little difficulty. Examples are occasionally seen in circulation. Likewise, with minimal persistence, the stuck digit can be procured on small size paper money. Both the partially turned digit and stuck digit errors have been observed on every class and denomination (through $100) of currency manufactured since the series of 1928. The errors appear most commonly on the $1 denomination and predominate on Federal Reserve notes (FRN) and SC. As with most mistakes, they prove more difficult to locate on the $2 denomination and on national currency, Federal Reserve bank notes, and gold certificates.

Stuck block letters exist only on FRN. As one might anticipate, in evaluating stuck versus partially turned block letters, the preponderance are partially turned. Thus far, the suffix has been overwhelmingly affected.

In sharp contrast to other errors, a greater percentage of known inverted block characters involve a star rather than a letter. The most abundant are the series of 1935-G $1 SC with motto. The notes come from plate position H. The lower left serial number begins with an inverted star prefix. Two other inverted star prefix errors both involve series of 1928 $100 FRN. Some of the notes from the Dallas and San Francisco districts end with inverted star suffixes on one or both serial numbers. Although initially subtle, the upside down solid green star does make a strong visual impact once noticed. In recent years, a series 1935-E $1 SC with an inverted star on the lower left serial number (*-D block) has been identified. On the series 1950-B a $20 replacement note has been identified with an inverted star in the lower left position.

Research by Peter Huntoon uncovered the use of an inverted M (instead of a W) as the prefix in the upper right serial number of a series of 1957 $1 SC. The E2 and E4 positions are affected. Only about two dozen serial numbers have been recorded, although logic dictates that additional examples remain to be discovered.

Insights and Incidents. To paraphrase a Vietnam War-era pop song, "where have all the collectors gone?"

Collectors-even novices-seem to be actively avoiding the stuck digit error. Not merely exercising benign neglect but, consciously ignoring it. Admittedly, stuck digits fail to provide much visual excitement. Nonetheless, the error is not especially common; an example belongs in every type collection of errors.

In a comparative sense (number of stuck digits seen versus total quantity of notes printed), I believe this mistake is relatively more plentiful on $1 SC than on $1 FRN.

In 1997 I distributed a cache of seventy five or so $1 FRN with a turned suffix letter. The lower one-half of the C suffix evidenced itself in the upper 50%. Until this group entered the marketplace, the error was definitely uncommon. Stuck and turned prefix letters remain rare.

My opinion-mentioned in the previous editions and reiterated here-is that stuck digits are of equal scarcity as the most common mismatched serial numbers (and occasionally a precursor to them) still rings true.

The astute collector can infrequently spot an inverted star prefix in a dealer's inventory without being labeled as such, particularly on the series of 1935-G $1 SC with motto. As in any specialty arena, knowledge truly reigns supreme.

There have been no recent releases of significant quantities of stuck digits—nor is there ever a surplus of them on the market at any given time. As such, the error seems underpriced relative to the availability, despite the lack of interest.

| $1 | SC | 1957 | Inverted block character; comparison photo with error illustrated on lower note | R-7 |
| | | Fine: $500 | EF: $1500 | CU: $2000 |

| $1 | FRN | 1977 | Stuck digit | R-4 |
| | Fine: $50 | | EF: $150 | CU: $250 |

$1	FRN	1981	Turned digit		R-1
Fine: $5		EF: $10		CU: $25	

$1	FRN	1988-A	Turned suffix		R-3
Fine: $25		EF: $50		CU: $100	

$5	USN	1953	Stuck digit	
Fine: $500		EF: $1000		CU: $1500

$10   NBN   1929   Stuck digit
       Fine: $1000   EF: $2500   CU: $4500

$20   FRN   1963   Stuck digit; star note   R-5
       Fine: $250   EF: $500   CU: $750

$100   FRN   1928   Inverted block character; star   R-8
       Fine: $2500   EF: $7500   CU: $12,500

PART FOUR

FOLDS and OTHER ERRORS

CUTTING ERRORS

GUTTER OR INTERIOR FOLDS

PRINTED OR EXTERIOR FOLDS

MISCELLANEOUS ERRORS

*Live and appreciate what you have,
but don't stop visualizing on the big
things you want to accomplish.*

- G. C. Mercado

CUTTING ERRORS

Cutting errors come in two distinct varieties. Both the precipitating cause and the resultant appearance are distinctly different. However, in both scenarios the mistake occurs after the currency stock correctly accepts the first, second, and third printings. The miscut arises during the terminal stages of production when the sixteen subject half-sheets are separated into two subject blocks and then into individual notes.

A cutting error generated by misalignment of the uncut sheets upon meeting the knives produces a batch of notes with identical mistakes. Typically, such an error contains most of a dominant primary note and varying degrees of a secondary note nestled within the confines of the dimensions prescribed for the class of paper money. A direct one to one ratio exists such that the greater the amount of the primary note missing, the greater the amount of secondary note visible. An entire spectrum of outcomes is possible. The division can range from the finished product exhibiting equal parts of the primary and secondary notes (and consequently possessing two different serial numbers) to a primary note with an abnormally wide margin or simply the design border of

the secondary note. The cutting error-unlike the faulty alignment mistake-demonstrates an equal amount of poor centering on both sides of the note. Not surprisingly, the value of this type of cutting error rests directly upon the amount of the secondary note present.

The alternate cause of the cutting error is a fold in the sheet at the time of cutting. This type most commonly involves a small section of the blank edge of the sheet folding over onto a corner of a note. When the flap opens, the corner assumes a "butterfly" or "bow tie" configuration; hence, these terms are sometimes utilized to describe this defect. In other instances, minor to massive portions of the currency sheet fold over creating notes that vary from the proper dimensions. Typically such miscuts will contain part of secondary and potentially tertiary notes.

Fractional notes. Any alleged cutting error on fractional currency must be viewed with suspicion. Whole and partial uncut sheets of various denominations and from different issues remain extent nearly one and one-half centuries after being printed. Therefore, little effort would be required to fabricate a spurious cutting error.

Large size notes. Numerous genuine examples of cutting errors exist on large size paper money. The author has inspected miscuts from the series of 1862 United States notes through the series of 1882 and 1902 national currency to the series of 1923 silver certificates (SC). Many examples demonstrate a retained butterfly fold of adjacent currency paper. An equal number possess a small strip of the secondary note adjacent to the bulk of the primary note. Despite the relative availability of minor cutting errors on large size paper money, truly significant examples prove incredibly difficult to locate. Although uncut sheets of large size notes may be found in certain sophisticated collections, because of their intrinsic value, pedigrees, and recorded serial numbers it seems unlikely that someone would sacrifice a sheet in an attempt to produce a spurious error.

The government delivered national currency to the individual bank, most often in the form of uncut sheets. Local tellers or secretaries severed the sheets into separate notes. In many cases, little regard for accuracy was executed. Numerous pieces of poorly cut large size national currency can be located without difficulty. As the cutting was performed outside of the Bureau of Engraving and Printing (BEP), such poorly cut notes do not qualify as errors.

Small size notes. No class of paper money issued since 1928 has escaped erroneous cutting. Minor cutting errors-those containing the design frame from an adjacent note-exist on every class of small size paper money. Every denomination through $1,000 contains documented examples. As one might anticipate, the most visually spectacular miscuts are limited to FRN.

In contrast to most situations, the butterfly shaped cutting error appears in a higher percentage of instances on blue, rather than green, seals. Although certainly available on the Federal Reserve notes (FRN), the corner protrusion exists more abundantly on SC.

Since the BEP resumed sales of uncut sheets to collectors, a prime opportunity for fraud and misrepresentation has emerged. Unscrupulous persons will purchase an uncut sheet, to generate pseudo-cutting errors by extracting segments of the sheet and incorporating portions of two or more notes. The dishonest then attempt to sell these fabrications to the unsuspecting public. Any purported cutting error on a series of 1976 $2 star note, series of 1981 or later $1, or recent issue $5, $10, $20, or $50 must be approached with caution. Although there has been some variability, in general, uncut sheets sold by the BEP begin with 98,640,000 or higher. If the serial number on the note in question meets or exceeds this, the piece is a fantasy alteration.

Insights and Incidents. Some legitimately phenomenal cutting errors continue to trade hands, both publicly and privately. Two stellar notes come to mind: a $1 and $20 FRN which exhibit a complete primary note, greater than 50% of a secondary note, and nearly 35% of a tertiary note. Such spectacular pieces arise from a huge, oblique fold on the uncut half-sheets after the application of the third print.

However, the most dramatic cutting error I've ever seen surfaced at a paper money show in Chicago in 1998. The magnificent piece arose from insertion of the half-sheet edge-instead of end-first into the cutting knives; a ninety degree mis-orientation. Although of proper dimensions, the note contains two portraits of Andrew Jackson perpendicular to the long axis of the paper! Compounding the magnificence was a BEP-applied rubber stamp, in purple ink, declaring "NO VALUE / RETURNED BY /BEP" within a rectangle. Of the innumerable alterations and additions seen, this blockbuster piece represents the lone example whereby application of a stamp actually enhances the value and desirability. The note-a series of 1985 $20 FRN from the Kansas City district-was submitted to the BEP by the teller who initially found it. Government employees stamped the note prior to returning it. This note later sold as part of the Taylor Family Collection, auctioned in February of 2005.

Collectors and dealers new to the error specialty continue to be duped by fraudulent cutting errors. Most disconcerting are those on modern $1, $2, $5, $10, $20, and $50 FRN sold in whole or partial sheet form by the BEP. The abundance of pieces altered for profit is sickening. Internet auctions make ideal outlets for disposing of these fabrications. A simple recollection of the facts concerning the serial numbers made available to collectors, in sheet form, would eliminate financial nightmares, emotional turmoil, and unscrupulous sellers. A quick rule of thumb: any $1 through $10 FRN after series of 1981 bearing a serial number greater than 98,640,00 must be suspect. While one must refine the rough parameters given here to more accurately assess a particular piece, a conservative collector generally cannot be led astray by adhering to these guidelines.

A case in point: in August, 1998 I was urged to take the next available flight to Puerto Rico to evaluate and purchase the "greatest collection of $5 errors." Through patient persistence I was able to eventually secure photocopies of some of the notes. A process which took entirely too long in the days of fax machines, e-mail, and overnight express. Every piece represented in the photocopies proved to be alterations from recently released uncut sheets of series of 1995 $5 FRN.

Although dramatic cutting errors certainly exist, the opportunity to acquire legitimate ones occurs infrequently. The collector must remain on guard against spurious fabrications. No dealer or auction house can be expert in all nuances of United States paper money. However, reputable firms permit an unqualified return in the event a piece is proven fake.

EXAMPLES OF THE ERROR

MINOR

MODERATE

MAJOR

$1   FRN   1977   Cutting error; major   R-6

      Fine: $500   EF: $1000   CU: $2000

$1   FRN   1977   Cutting error; major   R-6
                              consecutive pair: one too tall,
                              one too short

      Fine: $---   EF: $2000   CU: $3500

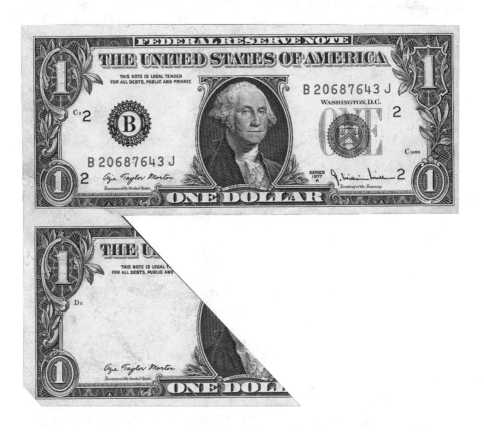

$1	FRN	1977-A	Cutting error; major	R-6
Fine: $---		EF: $2000		CU: $3500

$1	FRN	1977-A	Cutting error; major		R-6
	Fine: $---		EF: $2000	CU: $3500	

$1	FRN	1981	Cutting error; minor		R-1
	Fine: $50		EF: $150	CU: $250	

| $1 | FRN | 1981-A | Cutting error; moderate | R-5 |

Fine: $250   EF: $750   CU: $1250

| $1 | FRN | 1988-A | Cutting error; major | R-6 |

Fine: $500   EF: $1500   CU: $2500

| $2 | FRN | 1976 | Cutting error; major | R-7 |

Fine: $500   EF: $1000   CU: $2000

$2   FRN   1976   Cutting error; major   R-7

Fine: $---   EF: $2500   CU: $5000

| $5 | FRN | 1985 | Cutting error; moderate | R-5 |

Fine: $250   **EF: $500**   **CU: $750**

| $5 | FRN | 1988 | Cutting error; major | R-6 |

Fine: $---   **EF: $1500**   **CU: $2500**

| $5 | FRN | 1995 | Cutting error; moderate | R-5 |

Fine: $250   **EF: $750**   **CU: $1250**

$10   FRN   1988-A   Cutting error; major   R-6
        Fine: $---   EF: $3500   CU: $6500

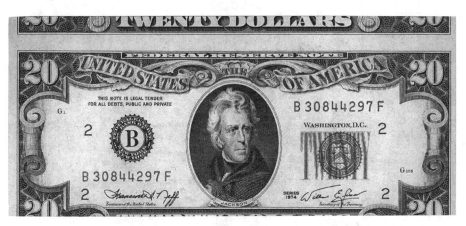

$20   FRN   1974   Cutting error; moderate   R-5

Fine: $250   **EF: $750**   **CU: $1250**

$20   FRN   1985   Cutting error; major   R-6

Fine: $---   **EF: $3500**   **CU: $6500**

$20	FRN	1985	Cutting error; major	R-6

Fine: $---   **EF: $3500**   **CU: $6500**

$20	FRN	1988-A	Cutting error; moderate	R-5

Fine: $---   **EF: $750**   **CU: $1250**

$50	FRN	1996	Cutting error; minor	R-4

Fine: $75   **EF: $150**   **CU: $250**

$100	FRN	1996	Cutting error; moderate		R-5
	Fine: $150		EF: $250	CU: $500	

$1000	FRN	1934-A	Cutting error; minor		R-4
	Fine: $5000		EF: $7500	CU: $15,000	

You don't concentrate on risks. You concentrate on results. No risk is too great to prevent the necessary job from getting done.

- Charles Yeager

GUTTER or INTERIOR FOLDS

Gutter or interior folds demonstrate a blank, unprinted, white channel interrupting the back, face, or over printing. Gutter folds develop when a double wrinkle occurs in the currency paper as it receives a printed image. The pleated area remains protected and continues devoid of an impression. With the pleat or fold intact and undisturbed from its position at the time of printing, no error is apparent. The design appears complete and the note seems to conform to appropriate dimensions. However, when the crease is opened, the characteristic white gutter disturbing the design becomes exposed.

Single gutter or interior folds involve an overlap of the paper caused by the wrinkle. Not too infrequently, numerous wrinkles occur yielding a note with multiple gutters that open accordion style. Single and multiple gutters may affect only the face or back or both surfaces of a note. Interior folds are relatively common on all types of United States paper money.

Gutter folds are the second most abundant error, lagging behind the ubiquitous ink smear mistake.

Fractional notes. Unquestionably, gutter folds represent the most common error on fractional currency. The author has examined nearly four dozen different examples—including those on uniface "specimens" designed to test new designs and plates. Undoubtedly, countless others exist in private and public holdings. Most are single interior folds affecting only one side of the note. However, a spectacular piece from the first issue, on a five cent value, exhibits several gutters on both sides.

Large size notes. Large size paper money contains far more gutter folds than most collectors and dealers realize. Although not as common as similar errors on small size notes, an interior fold on large size currency is not a rarity. Even accounting for the popularity of errors on large size notes, such errors are frequently overpriced when offered for sale. Gutter folds are known on all denominations between $1 and $20. These affect silver certificates (SC), gold certificates, United States notes, Federal Reserve bank notes, national currency, and Federal Reserve notes (FRN). Reliable sources report the existence of a gutter fold on series of 1914 $100 blue seal FRN.

Small size notes. Gutter folds are known on all classes of small size currency. Even the Federal Reserve bank notes, gold certificates, and national currency contain a sprinkling of examples. Among the FRN, this error can be confirmed on every denomination through the $1,000. Despite the relative availability of notes with a gutter fold, locating a truly dramatic piece with either one extremely wide gutter or with multiple interior folds remains a moderate challenge. Single gutter folds on circulated notes, especially on the $20 through $100 denominations, carry little collector premium. Many are spent at face value even by those aware of the mistake or languish in dealers' inventories for prolonged periods.

Insights and Incidents. A new slant in the retailing of gutter folds involves a price structure based upon the number of printing stages interrupted. An interior fold disrupting the back, face, and overprint carries a significant premium above a note wherein merely one or two printings are split. Intuitively, this approach to pricing makes sense. One can expect this trend to continue into the foreseeable future.

As the error field has matured into a distinct subspecialty within the general United States paper money market, collectors have become increasingly sophisticated. Today, far greater numbers of collectors recognize the rarity of the common gutter fold on uncommon host notes. These advanced collectors are prepared to pay appropriately to secure examples of the error on national currency, gold certificates, Federal Reserve bank notes, and the "Hawaii" and "North Africa" issues of World War II. Other collectors focus on obtaining gutter folds on star or replacement notes.

Once relegated to a second class status and dismissed as an unworthy error, unusual gutter folds now command appropriate recognition. Sophisticated collectors recognize the importance of securing interesting specimens for their enjoyment.

An anecdotal observation suggests that fewer gutter folds are escaping the BEP today, than in the past. Although the reason is unknown, this trend needs to be followed to be confirmed. If proven, the status of these lowly errors is likely to rise.

EXAMPLES OF THE ERROR

MINOR

MODERATE

MAJOR

$1   SC   1935-A   Gutter (interior) fold; single   R-1
Fine: $25   **EF: $50**   **CU: $100**

$1   SC   1935-E   Gutter (interior) fold; single   R-1
Fine: $10   **EF: $25**   **CU: $50**

$1   FRN   1969-B   Gutter (interior) fold; multiple   R-3
Fine: $25   **EF: $75**   **CU: $150**

$1	FRN	1985	Gutter (interior) fold; multiple	R-3
	Fine: $150		EF: $350	CU: $500

$1	FRN	2001	Gutter (interior) fold; single	R-1
	Fine: $750		EF: $2000	CU: $4500

$2	USN	1928-G	Gutter (interior) fold; single	
	Fine: $350		EF: $550	CU: $750

$2   USN   1953   Gutter (interior) fold; single
Fine: $75   **EF: $150**   **CU: $350**

$2   FRN   1976   Gutter (interior) fold; single   R-2
          Fine: $75   **EF: $150**   **CU: $350**

$5   FRN   1950-D   Gutter (interior) fold; star note   R-2
          Fine: $150   **EF: $200**   **CU: $300**

$5	FRN	1969	Gutter (interior) fold; single	R-1

Fine: $25   **EF: $50**   **CU: $75**

$5	FRN	1977-A	Gutter (interior) fold; multiple consecutive pair	R-3

Fine: $250   **EF: $500**   **CU: $750**

$5   FRN   1988-A   Gutter (interior) fold; major   R-3
Fine: $100   **EF: $250**   **CU: $450**

$5   FRN   1988-A   Gutter (interior) fold; major   R-3
Fine: $500   **EF: $1250**   **CU: $2500**

$5   FRN   1988-A   Gutter (interior) fold; major   R-3
Fine: $500   **EF: $1000**   **CU: $1500**

| $5 | FRN | 1995 | | Gutter (interior) fold; major | R-3 |
| | **Fine: $100** | | **EF: $250** | | **CU: $450** |

| $5 | FRN | 1995 | | Gutter (interior) fold; single | R-1 |
| | **Fine: $25** | | **EF: $35** | | **CU: $75** |

| $10 | GC | 1928 | | Gutter (interior) fold; single |
| | **Fine: $1000** | | **EF: $2500** | | **CU: $3500** |

$10	FRN	1950-A	Gutter (interior) fold; multiple	R-3
Fine: $50			**EF: $100**	**CU: $200**

$10	FRN	1990	Gutter (interior) fold; moderate	R-3
Fine: $100			**EF: $150**	**CU: $250**

$20	FRN	1985	Gutter (interior) fold; major	R-3
Fine: $100			**EF: $250**	**CU: $450**

| $20 | FRN | 1996 | Gutter (interior) fold; major | R-3 |

Fine: $100   EF: $250   CU: $500

| $50 | FRN | 1963-A | Gutter (interior) fold; single | R-1 |

Fine: $75   EF: $100   CU: $150

| $100 | FRN | 1993 | Gutter (interior) fold; major | R-3 |

Fine: $250   EF: $750   CU: $1500

$100 FRN 1996 Gutter (interior) fold; moderate R-3
Fine: $150 EF: $200 CU: $300

$500 FRN 1934-A Gutter (interior) fold; minor R-1
Fine: $2500 EF: $3500 CU: $5000

$1000 FRN 1934-A Gutter (interior) fold; minor R-1
Fine: $3500 EF: $5000 CU: $8500

Never look back unless you are planning to go that way.
No man is rich enough to buy back his past.

- Oscar Wilde

PRINTED or EXTERIOR FOLDS

Printed or exterior folds demonstrate a portion of the design intended for one side printed on the opposite side of the note. Currency paper is subject to being folded along the entire route from blank sheet to finished product. Whenever a section of the sheet folds over onto itself prior to or during contact with a printing plate, a printed fold error ensues. The sheet may remain folded after the printing or open prior to subsequent, if any, printing operations and the cutting knives. The ultimate shape of the note depends upon whether the sheet unfolds before being cut.

Minor exterior folds-such as those that affect one corner-appear with moderate frequency. Large printed folds involving a major percentage of a note exist in very limited numbers. Especially elusive are major printed folds where the sheet folded between the back and face printing and opened prior to the application of the third print. This striking mistake includes a portion of the face design atop the already present back. When unfolded, a portion of the serial numbers and/or seals rest against a stark white background which was protected during the second print.

Notes which remain folded for the cutting and banding operations enter banking channels and public circulation demonstrating an irregular shape when unfolded. Obviously the more visually alluring the specimen, the greater the value.

Fractional notes. Locating a printed fold on fractional currency requires years of diligence and a dose of luck. The author has examined three such pieces during the past two to three decades. There are unconfirmed reports of two other printed folds on these Civil War substitutes for paper money. Even the tiniest example represents an enormous find.

Large size notes. Exterior folds on large size paper money are prohibitively rare. Of the seven pieces examined, one is especially memorable. The lower right corner of a series of 1880 $5 United States note (USN) folded upward capturing most of the large seal. The piece originally sold publicly in the Albert A. Grinnell auctions during the 1940s. It was auctioned again in 2005. Although not on quite the same level, there are moderate printed folds on at least two different examples of series 1923 $1 silver certificates (SC), and less dramatic examples on series 1917 $1 USN and series 1918 $1 Federal Reserve bank notes (FRBN). Any example of a printed fold on large size paper money should be a highly cherished trophy.

Small size notes. The most spectacular examples exist on Federal Reserve notes (FRN) of the series of 1977 and later. The printed fold error is known on all denominations of FRN from $1 through $1000. There remain four documented examples on series of 1928 gold certificates; three involve the $10 denomination, the other a $20. None are confirmed on Federal Reserve bank notes. Approximately two dozen are reported on national currency. Of the small size silver certificates and USN, the former offer roughly six times as many opportunities to obtain an example than the later, although truly dramatic examples are confined to the SC.

Insights and Incidents. When my father-a professional numismatist with four and one-half decades of experience-located a printed fold on a piece of fractional currency in 1996, I advertised it as "possibly unique." However, the fickle finger of fate turned sharply against me. Within twelve months, a few more pieces entered the marketplace. All originated with the Milton Friedberg collection sold by Currency Auctions of America. Even "experts" must revise their opinions in a dynamic market with ever-changing facts. Nonetheless, whether described as "unique", "possibly unique," or "nearly unique" (an oxymoron), printed folds on fractional currency remain genuinely rare.

Since the publication of the first two editions, a few other printed folds on large size paper money have crept out of the woodwork and into the census. One piece carries a particularly interesting history. It is a series of 1917 $1 USN with a minor to moderate fold over affecting the lower left corner of the face. The flap caught a portion of the second print. The piece had been displayed under two-sided glass since it was extracted from circulation during the Great Depression.

Truly amazing printed folds, on small size notes, filter into the marketplace at a rate of about one every six months. While some collectors perceive these stunning specimens to be priced too high, others relish the privilege to add such incredible notes to their holdings. Perception remains critical. Yet, the collector who perceives that fairly priced examples cost too much will never own one worthy of bragging rights.

EXAMPLES OF THE ERROR

MINOR

MODERATE

MAJOR

$1	SC	1928-B	Printed fold; moderate		R-5
	Fine: $500		EF: $1000	CU: $1500	

$1	FRN	1969-D	Printed fold; major		R-7
	Fine: $250		EF: $750	CU: $1500	

$1	FRN	1974	Printed tear; major		R-7
	Fine: $250		EF: $750	CU: $1500	

$1	FRN	1981	Printed tear; major		R-7
	Fine: $500		EF: $1500	CU: $2500	

$1	FRN	1981-A	Printed tear; major		R-7
	Fine: $500		EF: $1000	CU: $2000	

$2	USN	1953	Printed fold; moderate	
	Fine: $1000		EF: $2000	CU: $3500

$2	FRN	1976	Printed fold; moderate	R-6
	Fine: $500		**EF: $1500**	**CU: $2500**

$5	SC	1934-A	Printed fold; major	R-7
	Fine: $500		**EF: $1000**	**CU: $2000**

$5	SC	1953	Printed fold; moderate	R-5
	Fine: $250		**EF: $750**	**CU: $1500**

$5	FRN	1977-A	Printed fold; major	R-7
Fine: $250		**EF: $750**		**CU: $1500**

$5	FRN	1977-A	Printed fold; minor	R-4
Fine: $100		**EF: $250**		**CU: $450**

$5	FRN	1977-A	Printed fold; moderate	R-5
Fine: $100		**EF: $250**		**CU: $500**

$5	FRN	1981	Printed fold; moderate		R-5
	Fine: $150		EF: $350	CU: $650	

$10	FRN	1977-A	Printed fold; moderate		R-5
	Fine: $150		EF: $350	CU: $650	

$10	FRN	1981	Printed fold; moderate		R-5
	Fine: $150		EF: $350	CU: $650	

$10   FRN   1981   Printed fold; major   R-7
       Fine: $500   EF: $1000   CU: $2000

$20   FRN   1981   Printed fold; moderate   R-5
       Fine: $100   EF: $250   CU: $500

$20   FRN   1993   Printed fold; major   R-7
       Fine: $500   EF: $1000   CU: $1500

$20	FRN	1993	Printed fold; major	R-7

Fine: $500   **EF: $1000**   **CU: $2000**

$20	FRN	1995	Printed fold; major	R-7

Fine: $1000   **EF: $2000**   **CU: $3500**

$20	FRN	1996	Printed fold; major	R-7

Fine: $500   **EF: $1000**   **CU: $2000**

| $50 | FRN | 1985 | Printed fold; moderate | | R-5 |
| | Fine: $250 | | EF: $750 | CU: $1500 | |

| $100 | FRN | 1988 | Printed fold; moderate | | R-5 |
| | Fine: $250 | | EF: $750 | CU: $1500 | |

| $100 | FRN | 1996 | Printed fold; minor | | R-4 |
| | Fine: $150 | | EF: $350 | CU: $750 | |

Life is no brief candle to me. It is a sort of splendid torch which I have got a hold of for the moment, and I want to make it burn as brightly as possible before handing it on to future generations.

-George Bernard Shaw

MISCELLANEOUS ERRORS

This chapter addresses several different types of mistakes. These miscellaneous errors cannot be compartmentalized conveniently into other categories. The varieties included are the:

- end of roll error,
- mixed denomination sets,
- wrong stock error,
- engraving errors,
- printed scrap,
- transposed currency stock,
- missing magnetic ink,
- watermark variations,
- pre-printed stock,
- district designator variances, and
- defective stock.

The **end of roll error** originates from markings or splices created by Crane and Co. This firm supplies the Bureau of Engraving and Printing (BEP) with currency stock. Markings take various forms. Until recently, an impregnated red or purple diagonal line indicated the end of the roll. Since the series of 1990, a matte green indicator strip forewarns the press operator. When the matte green marked paper is accidentally utilized for currency production, the marking appears vertically at one end usually correlating with a faulty alignment on the opposite side. The more exciting (and expensive) variety of the end of roll error is the retained splice. Splices occur at the paper production facility. The mill adjoins several strips of paper to create a roll that meets BEP contract specifications. A turquoise-color double sided water soluble tape is currently utilized to connect the independent sheets forming the enormous roll. At the BEP, as the roll is cut into individual sheets before the first printing, electronic sensors scan the roll. The sensors should identify the splices and the alert the workmen to extract and discard that portion of the paper. When the sensors fail, the paper enters currency production. The final product will assume a double thickness, from the overlap of the ends of the sheets united to form the roll. Characteristically, one edge will be feathered. Since the publication of the first two editions, numerous end of roll errors have reached circulation—and been enthusiastically received by the collecting community.

Mixed denomination sets occur when a sheet of stock prepared for one denomination becomes mixed within a stack of sheets for another denomination and the entire group enters the overprinting press. Caution must be exercised as this can be replicated outside of government facilities. One can intermingle notes from two packs of different denominations with the same serial numbers.

There are six documented sets of mixed denomination notes. One is a series of 1974 $20 Federal Reserve note (FRN) found in a pack of series of 1976 $2 denominations from the Chicago district. At least two of these are known. Another set is a $10-$20-$10 combination from the series of 1974 FRN on the Richmond district. This trio can unhesitatingly be declared genuine because BEP documents confirm that the serial number on the $20 note was previously printed on a series of 1969-C FRN in August of 1974. The $10 notes with which the $20 was found were printed exactly two years later. This set was reported by Harry Forman and reported in a February, 1977 article in *Coin World*. The third mixed denomination set encompasses a sequential run of twelve notes from the series of 1990. The first four notes are of the (correct) $20 denomination, the intervening four notes bear the $50 denomination, and the final pieces revert to the $20 value. Stephen M. Sullivan reported a mixed denomination pair from the series of 1977 from the Boston district. The lower numbered note, a $1, is sequential to a $5 FRN. Apparently the error was documented prior to the serial number actually being used

on the $5 denomination. The most recently recorded mixed denomination set comes from the Chicago district and involves two sequential $10 notes from the serial of 1988-A followed by two consecutive $20 notes from the series of 1990. Additional data appear in the table on mixed denomination sets.

The **wrong stock error** shares the elite stratum with the rarest of paper money mistakes. The wrong stock error carries the first and second printing of one type of currency and the overprint of another. These ultra-rarities occurred during periods when the BEP was producing more than one class of currency simultaneously; specifically from the mid-1950s through the early-1960s. There are three separate varieties documented. One transitional piece involves a series of 1957-B silver certificate (SC) overprinted with a black Federal Reserve seal and district numbers plus green serial numbers and Treasury seal. Another subset, of which two specimens exist, is the series of 1950 $5 FRN with the blue overprint of the series of 1953 SC. The final piece is a series of 1950-B $5 FRN demonstrating a red overprint from the series of 1953 United States note (USN).

Some authorities postulate that the series of 1988-A $1 FRN printed on a web press created by the Hamilton-Stevens Company of Ohio and subsequently overprinted with a star suffix for the Atlanta district qualify as wrong stock errors. As the intended overprint for all web notes was thestandard currency overprinting and processing equipment already in place for overprinting FRN, this particular variety-however interesting and collectible-fails to satisfy the criteria for the wrong stock error. In this instance, a FRN (albeit manufactured on different equipment) received the overprint of a FRN. Although the BEP indicated it did not plan to issue star or replacement notes on web-fed host notes, it nonetheless did so inadvertently.

Since the publication of the second edition, an important wrong stock error has come to light. It is a series 1995 $1 with a fragment of a TEN DOLLAR security thread embedded into the substance of the paper stock.

Engraving errors represent mistakes in the production of plates employed to print paper money. As such, these irregularities are the fault of the BEP engraver. Few currency errors originate with the engravers. Engraving errors remain significantly different than most of the mistakes addressed in this book which result from mechanical problems.

A vast spectrum of engraving errors plague United States paper money, both large and small size. Numerous denominations and types exist. The most famous engraving error on large size currency involves the transposed locations of the engraved signatures of William Elliott and John Burke on the series of 1917 $1 USN. The mistake shows the engraved signature of Burke, on the left, over the position for the registrar of the Treasury and

the signature of Elliott, on the right, above the designator for the treasurer of the United States. The engraving error affects face plate number 1519 only.

An engraving error-which exists in greater supply than most realize-appears on the series of 1907 $5 USN. In particular, the Speelman-White signature combination of the so-called "woodchopper family" design. The obligation, engraved on the back, reads "for all debts PCBLIC and private." To the unaided eye the error is obvious.

A subtle engraving error appears on the series of 1899 $1 SC. Below the engraved signature of Charles H. Treat, the title Treasurer of the United States reads "Treasurer of the United State." lacking the final "s" and concluding with a period. The engraving error affects face plate 2985 in the check position B only.

Another difficult to appreciate engraving error exists on the series of 1886 $5 SC. This type is often called the "silver dollar back", as five Morgan dollars comprise the back design. This error was identified during a time when interest in paper money mistakes seemed virtually non-existent. More than a century ago, Joseph Hooper, writing in the March, 1896 volume of The Numismatist, observed that "The third one of these (silver dollars) from the left end of the certificate has the word TRUST spelled TRAST. On all the others the word is properly spelled."

Research by Peter Huntoon on proof

impressions of uncut sheets in government archives unearthed another engraving error on large size paper money. This particular example is a series of 1902 $20 national currency from The First National Bank of Oxnard, California, bank charter number 9481. The signature of Charles H. Treat appears twice; once (correctly) over the Treasurer of the United States and also above the Register's position. Although printed on a bi-denominational sheet, with a $10-$10-$10-$20 configuration, the engraving error affects the $20 denomination with check position A only.

Another discovery by Huntoon is the mirror –placement of back plate check number 46 on the series 1902 Date Backs for the $10 denomination. The engraver placed the number in the lower left corner of the back, instead of the correct location on the lower right. The plate was used for one month in 1913 and undoubtedly issued notes exist, waiting to be identified.

Among national currency, the First National Bank of L'Anse Creuse, Michigan, Charter-12661 has the incorrect date engraved into the plate. It reads February 16, 1924; when the correct yar was 1925.

On small size paper money, several engraving errors are confirmed. Certainly one of the most popular is the series of 1928 $2 USN produced without a back plate number. Research by pioneering small size currency specialist Chuck O'Donnell suggests the correct number should be plate 100.

However, others have disputed this claim. Although most circulated unnoticed, a fair supply still exists in uncirculated condition to satisfy the demands of modern error collectors. One can occasionally locate a generic specimen which has not been attributed as an error. Three star or replacement notes lacking the back plate number on this issue are recorded.

A bona fide rarity on small size paper money concerning engraving errors occurs on the series of 1928 $10 gold certificates. At least five examples are known without a face plate number. The author has examined three or four of the specimens and found no evidence of tampering.

Another subtle mistake that involves the back plate number occurs on the series of 1974 $1 FRN. The back plate reads 905, instead of 1905. The correct back plate 905 was last used seven years before the production of these The Atlanta and St. Louis districts carry examples affecting the F-D and H-A blocks, respectively. The incorrect back plate was mated with at least five different face plates.

Another engraving error from the series 1974 $1 denomination is the use of an intermediate size back plate. The mistake only affects the right-half of the thirty-two subject sheet. The left-half contains back check numbers of correct size. Examples are known from both Philadelphia and Dallas, but undoubtedly additional districts were affected.

The BEP resumed public sales of uncut sheets of paper money with the series of 1981 $1 FRN-and immediately released an engraving error. The mistake appears on the thirty-two subject sheets, from the E-E block. The back plate error reads 7273, instead of the correct 3273. The engraving error affects plate position H1 only.

Undoubtedly the most abundant engraving error appears on the series of 1981-A and 1985 $1 FRN. The mis-engraved back plate was utilized during the summer months of 1985 amidst the time frame when the BEP was in transition from 1981-A to 1985. Approximately three million pieces were printed and released with an improperly positioned back plate number. The number was engraved beneath the "O" in "ONE" on the left side of the back, rather than below the "E" on the right. This error exists in every one of the thirty two positions from the back plate cylinder. For the series of 1981-A, the back plate 129 error has been recorded on the Philadelphia, St. Louis, Minneapolis, and San Francisco districts. On the series of 1985, all districts are confirmed, with the exception of Philadelphia, Minneapolis, Kansas City and Dallas. Additional data appear in the table on back plate 129 engraving errors.

Since the opening of the Forth Worth (Texas) facility of the BEP, notes printed there are distinguished by two characteristics. First, the initials "FW" precede the face check letter and face plate number in the lower right corner of the front. Second, the back check number measures 1mm; whereas, notes printed at the Washington, D.C. headquarters show back check numbers 0.6mm in height. There is a similar disparity in size on the face check numbers with the Washington, D.C. indicators predictably larger. For the series of 1988-A, an engraving error exists on face plate 106 for the Fort Worth facility. The check number is too large, matching the correct size for Washington, D.C. This occurred only for the San Francisco district for notes printed in June and July of 1991. For the series 1995, a staggering quantity of $1 FRN produced at the Forth Worth facility was released with back plate numbers of the smaller size. The error affects twelve blocks from six different districts. Star or replacement notes-issued only on the Chicago district-are especially rare. The error affects back plate number 295 only. Additional data appear in the table on back plate 295 engraving errors.

Another wrong size engraving error is the face plate 106 found on series 1988-A $1 from San Francisco. A larger font size was employed to create the check number. Interestingly, the large font actually belonged to a back plate size from Fort Worth production facility. The error has been found on the L-D, L-E, L-F, and L-* blocks.

Among national currency the American National Bank at Indianapolis, Indiana, Charter-13759 has the word "of" typeset between Bank and Indianapolis (instead of "at") on most of the early emissions from the institution. In fact, it is easier to find examples with the mistaken title rather than with the corrected one.

The *printed scrap mistake* occurs extremely infrequently. Generally, one considers scrap to be paper other than that intended for currency production. However, fragments of currency stock that accidentally enter the printing press also qualify as printed scrap. Most often the scrap, typically of smaller size than issued notes, falls to the floor as the pallets of paper money are moved from station to station. All examples are tremendously rare outside of the BEP. The few known pieces of printed scrap arose from small size FRN. In an era of uncut sheets being publicly available, one must verify beyond doubt that an offered item reflects a genuine printed scrap error.

A fascinating-and extremely rare-variety of the printed scrap error encompasses overprints on sizing paper. There are three verified examples. In each, an entire third print rests on bright white sizing paper. The paper appears so markedly different from typically currency stock that no room for confusion exists. One of the specimens demonstrates a faint offset from a $20 FRN, exposing its origin. The overprinted sizing paper and intended host note, if recovered together, might also be classified as an obstructed print with retained fragment.

The *transposed currency stock error* represents a fairly recent phenomenon. Effective with the series of 1990 $100 FRN, the BEP began to incorporate a polymer thread in the currency stock before printing. The security strip-which bears alternating numerals indicative of the denomination and the abbreviation USA-reflects one of many anti-counterfeiting devices. Beginning with the redesigned series of 1996 $100 FRN a watermark matching the portrait-was introduced to United States paper money. These blind devices dictate the orientation of the currency stock when it encounters the printing press. To facilitate alignment at the BEP, employees of Crane and Company notch the sheets prior to delivery. If the stack is marked incorrectly or if the pie-shaped cut is misinterpreted, the subsequent designs will vary in position relative to the security strip or watermark. Until such devices were instituted, it made no difference how the paper stock was positioned for the back printing.

Two distinct varieties exist. One simply involves the right to left end transposition of the sheets prior to the printing stages. The final product demonstrates the security thread and/or watermark on the wrong side(s). A more complicated happenstance occurs when the currency stock is rotated bottom to top before the printings. The resultant security features will appear with the polymer security thread on the incorrect side plus the watermark inverted on the other end of the note. Although seemingly unlikely, the BEP admits to printing 320,000 series of 1996 $100 FRN with the transposed security thread and inverted watermark. Most bear the New York district designator; a far lesser number carry the Cleveland marking. As these errors possess no eye appeal-in fact, the error remains obscure until held to a light source-they are unpopular with collectors.

The **missing magnetic ink** error began with the series of 1990 FRN, when the BEP instituted numerous anti-counterfeiting changes. Among the alterations was the use of magnetic ink, in a checkerboard pattern, on the face of the notes. Regular, non-magnetic ink completes the second print image. Approximately 35% of the face printing comes from magnetic ink. When the entire checkerboard pattern of magnetic ink is lacking, an attractive and desirable error ensues. Should only a portion of the magnetic ink fail to imprint-typically affecting the left end-collectors become less enthusiastic. The author has verified partial or complete patterns of missing magnetic ink on $5, $10, $20, $50, and $100 FRN.

Watermark variations exist because the security feature, initiated with the series of 1996 and later redesigned FRN, is embedded while the paper stock still consists of greater than 50% water during production at Crane and Company. As the currency stock dries at the mill, slight variations in the appearance of the president's portrait, who appears in the watermark, are possible. Although interesting, these minor variations attract nearly zero interest from collectors. As these watermark variations fall within normal quality control parameters, they do not technically qualify as errors.

Pre-printed stock examples remain exceedingly rare. To qualify as a pre-printed stock error, the first, second, or third printing must rest on top of an underlying (and extraneous) image. Authentication is best performed with the aid of magnification. A mere three specimens-all on modern $20 FRN-exist. A series of 1990 demonstrates an inexplicable chevron pattern imprinted into the stock before the application of the second or third printings. The note surfaced in Tallassee, Alabama. A series of 1995 contains precise circles of black coloration in multiple locations on both the face and back. Adding intrigue to the note is the co-existence of the overprint on the back. Finally, a series of 1996 exhibits a bold, retrograde impression of a bar code and control numbers underneath the portrait oval and the upper left serial number. Although many purported pre-printed stock errors arise, the critical element of BEP printings resting atop a pre-existing impression is lacking.

The **district designator variance** represents the latest error uncovered. In February and March of 2001, a handful of series 1999 $20 FRN came to light bearing an incorrect type (size) on the district letter-number combination beneath the upper right serial number. All currently verified examples originated with either the BD-A or BD-B block and face plates 1, 2, 3, 4, 5, 6, and 8. The black D4 designator measures 3mm (versus normal of 3.5mm) on the errors. Although seemingly a minor difference, the variation stands out impressively. The rarity and desirability of this error will be determined in the next few years. Thus far, no star replacement notes (BD-*) have been identified with variance in the district designator.

Defective stock occurs when the sludge used to create a roll of paper intended for currency production is rolled out unevenly. The pulp should be uniform in thickness when compressed. Irregularities in pulp thickness create variations in the thickness of the final stock. Theoretically, defective stock could involve a product which is too thick, although roller pressure doesn't allow excess clumps. In practice, defective stock errors involve paper money with portions of the paper which are too thin—in rare instances, the stock is so thin as to be translucent.

TABLE of MIXED DENOMINATION SETS

Denomination	Type	Series	Serial number	Catalog number
$10	FRN	1974	E 01300024 C	KL-2226, Fr-2022
$20	FRN	1974	E 01300025 C	KL-2503, Fr-2071
$10	FRN	1974	E 01300026 C	KL-2226, Fr-2022
$2	FRN	1976	G 28949988 A	KL-1633, Fr-1935
$20	FRN	1974	G 28949989 A	KL-2505, Fr-2071
$2	FRN	1976	G 28949990 A	KL-1633, Fr-1935
$1	FRN	1977	A 88585910 A	KL-1585, Fr-1909
$5	FRN	1977	A 88585911 A	KL-1936, Fr-1974
$10	FRN	1988-A	G 13774043 C	KL-3875, Fr-2028
$10	FRN	1988-A	G 13774044 C	
$20	FRN	1990	G 13774045 C	KL-3958, Fr-2077
$20	FRN	1990	G 13774046 C	
$20	FRN	1990	K 14174901 A	KL-3962, Fr-2078
$20	FRN	1990	K 14174902 A	
$20	FRN	1990	K 14174903 A	
$20	FRN	1990	K 14174904 A	
$50	FRN	1990	K 14174905 A	KL-3974, Fr-2124
$50	FRN	1990	K 14174906 A	
$50	FRN	1990	K 14174907 A	
$50	FRN	1990	K 14174908 A	
$20	FRN	1990	K 14174909 A	KL-3962, Fr-2078
$20	FRN	1990	K 14174910 A	
$20	FRN	1990	K 14174911 A	
$20	FRN	1990	K 14174912 A	

TABLE OF BACK PLATE 129 ENGRAVING ERRORS

Denomination	Type	Series	Block	Catalog number
$1	FRN	1981-A	C-A	KL-3602-A, Fr-1912 (Philadelphia)
			H-B	KL-3607-A, (St. Louis) (1)
			I-A	KL-3608-A, (Minneapolis)
			I-B	(Minneapolis) (2)
			L-G	KL-3611-A, (San Francisco)
		1985	A-A	KL-3700-A, Fr-1913 (Boston)
			B-A	KL-37001-A (New York)
			B-B	
			D-A	KL-3703-A (Cleveland)
			E-A	KL-3704-A (Richmond) (1)
			F-A	KL-3705-A (Atlanta)
			G-A	KL-3706-A (Chicago)
			H-A	KL-3707-A (St. Louis)
			J-A	KL-3709-A (Kansas City)
			K-A	KL-3710-A (Dallas) L-A
				KL-3711-A (San Francisco)

(1) most common block for the series
(2) rarest block for back plate 129 engraving errors

TABLE OF FORT WORTH 295 MICRO BACK PLATE NUMBERS

Denomination	Type	Series	Block	Catalog number
$1	FRN	1995	G-*	KL-4090*, Fr-1922-* (Chicago)
			G-M	KL-4090, Fr-1922 G-N (1)
			H-E	KL-4091, (St. Louis)
			I-F	KL-4092, (Minneapolis) (1)
			I-G	
			I-H	
			J-F	KL-4093, (Kansas City)
			K-I	KL-4094, (Dallas)
			K-J	
			L-W	KL-4095, (San Francisco)(1)
			L-X	

(1) common block; the micro back plate mated with at least seventeen different face plates

$5   FRN   1981-A   End of roll; failed splice   R-8
      Fine: $---   EF: $5000   CU: $10,000

$10   FRN   1969-A   End of roll; matte stripe   R-8
      Fine: $250   EF: $500   CU: $1000

$100   FRN   1996   End of roll; matte stripe   R-8
      Fine: $250   EF: $500   CU: $1000

$10-$20   FRN   1988-A-1990   Mixed denomination set   R-9

Fine: $---   EF: $5000   CU: $10,000

$5	FRN	1953	Wrong stock;	R-9

silver certificate overprint

Fine: $35,000   **EF: $50,000**   **CU: $---**

$1	FRN	1995	Wrong stock;	R-9

security thread from $10 embedded

Fine: $2500   **EF: $5,000**   **CU: $10,000**

$10	GC	1928	Engraving error; missing front check number	
	Fine: $1000		EF: $1500	CU: $2500

$1	FRN	1981-A	Engraving error; back plate 129 left side	R-4
	Fine: $25		EF: $50	CU: $100

| $1 | FRN | 1995 | Engraving error; back plate 295 micro size | R-4 |

Fine: $10   **EF: $25**   **CU: $50**

$5   FRN   1969-C   Printed scrap   R-9

Fine: $500   **EF: $1500**   **CU: $2500**

| $100 | FRN | 1990 | Missing magnetic ink | | R-5 |
| | Fine: $250 | | EF: $500 | CU: $1500 | |

| $20 | FRN | 1993 | Missing non-magnetic ink | | R-5 |
| | Fine: $250 | | EF: $500 | CU: $1000 | |

| $20 | FRN | 1996 | Pre-printed stock | R-9 |

Fine: **$2500**   EF: **$4500**   CU: **$6500**

| $20 | FRN | 1999 | District designator variance; comparison illustration, error on lower note | R-8 |

Fine: **$250**   EF: **$500**   CU: **$750**

$1	FRN	1981	Defective stock	R-9

Fine: $1000   **EF: $2500**   **CU: $3500**

$1	FRN	1981	Identical serial numbers	R-9

Fine: $---   **EF: $7500**   **CU: $15,000**

EPILOGUE

He said I was in my early forties
with a lot of life before me
when a moment came that stopped me on a dime
and I spent most of the next days
looking at the x-rays
Talking bout the options
and talking bout sweet time
I asked him when it sank in
that this might really be the real end
how's it hit you when you get that kinda news
man what'd you do?

And he said
I went sky diving
I went Rocky Mountain climbing
I went 2.7 seconds on a bull named Fu Man Chu
and I loved deeper and I spoke sweeter
and I gave forgiveness I'd been denying
and he said someday I hope you get the chance
to live like you were dying.

He said I was finally the husband
that most the time I wasn't
and I became a friend a friend would like to have
and all the sudden going fishin
wasn't such an imposition
and I went three times that year I lost my dad
well I finally read the good book
and I took a good long hard look
at what I'd do if I could do it all again

And then
I went sky diving
I went Rocky Mountain climbing
I went 2.7 seconds on a bull named Fu Man Chu
and I loved deeper and I spoke sweeter
and I gave forgiveness I'd been denying

and he said someday I hope you get the chance
to live like you were dying.

Like tomorrow was a gift and you got eternity to think about
What'd you do with it what did you do with it
what did I do with it
what would I do with it?

--Tim Nichols, Craig Michael Wiseman, Tim McGraw

[Numismatics]…was his life;
it was not his livelihood.
And it made him feel so happy
and it made him feel so good.

\- Harry Chapin

ABOUT the AUTHOR

After receiving a medical degree, Fredrick J. Bart completed a post-graduate surgical residency under the auspices of the Johns Hopkins Hospital and a subsequent one year fellowship. The author lectured extensively throughout North America to other surgeons and published nearly forty articles in the medical literature. He spent a decade performing emergency and elective reconstructive surgery before changing the focus of his attention.

Frederick J. Bart enjoys a wide spectrum of interests. He has completed several marathons, each of 26.2 miles in length. He is a certified SCUBA diver and a high school level referee for soccer. Among other life-defining experiences, Frederick J. Bart served as a Torchbearer for the 2002 Olympic Games in Salt Lake City.

He has travelled to Africa twice, for plains game safaris. He has pursued caribou with Inuit Eskimos in the arctic tundra, black bear in remote Alberta under the northern lights, record book antelope on the plains of Wyoming, elk in mountains infested with grizzly bear, wild boar in southern swamps, and other species. His love of the outdoors draws him to bow hunting .

Frederick J. Bart is recognized as an authority on United States paper money errors. Interviews with him have appeared on NBC television as well as CNN. He has been quoted in USA Today, numerous newspapers throughout the country, and extensively in the numismatic publications. He formed the finest collection of small size errors on the $5 denomination. The collection was dispersed in 1998, as it offered little room for improvement. He collects serial number one national bank notes by state, large size serial number one notes, and exotic errors prior to 1963.

The author holds membership in the Professional Numismatists Guild, American Numismatic Association, Professional Currency Dealers Association, plus numerous regional and state organizations.

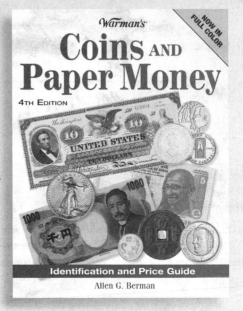
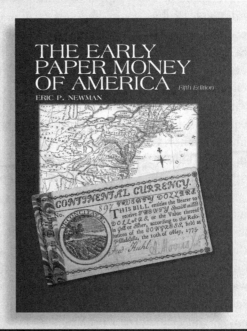

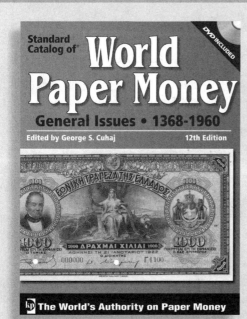

More Paper Money Details

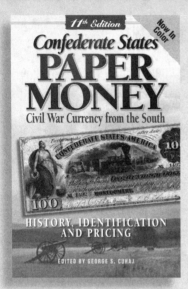

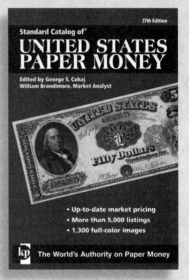

Confederate States Paper Money

Civil War Currency from the South

11th Edition
Edited by George S. Cuhaj

Engaging, easy-to-use and easy-to-carry, this guide reads like an intriguing Civil War tale, while providing updated market values and identifying data for Confederate and Southern States issues including uncut sheets, advertising notes, and errors.

Softcover • 6 x 9 • 272 pages
50 b&w phtos • 350 color photos

Item# Z2407 • $27.99

Standard Catalog of® United States Paper Money

27th Edition
Edited by George S. Cuhaj;
William Brandimore, Market Analyst

Concise, compact and in full-color, this new edition of the only paper money reference is easy to use and features 1,300 large-size color photos and current pricing.

Softcover • 6 x 9 • 432 pages
50 b&w photos • 1,300 color photos

Item# Z2408 • $26.99